"Maps can be useful if traveling with purpose on purpose. Based on the p[...] mitment therapy (ACT), this workbook provides step-by-step activities and [...] that keep those who create and use them on course—even when their journey gets difficult! Those who want to do more of what they most deeply hold to be worth doing will benefit from working their way through this book."

—**Hank Robb, PhD, ABPP**, peer-reviewed ACT trainer, fellow of the Association for
Contextual Behavioral Science, and author of *Willingly ACT for Spiritual Development*

"*Finding Your Why and Finding Your Way* provides a wide range of powerful life skills and exercises, written in a warm and engaging tone. It's full of relatable examples and engaging case studies that help increase self-insight into one's own behavior and potential barriers to creating change. If you want to identify what you care about, and develop a plan to attain your goals, this is a great resource."

—**Tamar D. Black, PhD**, educational and developmental psychologist, and
author of *ACT for Treating Children*

"Wounded Warrior Project uses ACT to help our warriors increase their resiliency and mental well-being. We are grateful to D.J. Moran and Siri Ming who have developed an innovative approach to ACT that is easily digestible to the warriors we serve through our Project Odyssey programs."

—**Joe Fox**, Project Odyssey Training Specialist at Wounded Warrior Project;
and Sergeant First Class, US Army, Ret.

"A superb, easy-to-read, and elegantly practical guide to building and enjoying a rich and meaningful life. The authors take you gently, step by step, through a journey of courage, compassion, and wonder—giving you all the skills and knowledge you'll need to make your life meaningful and fulfilling. One of the things I found incredibly refreshing in this book is the engaging, down-to-earth language; if (like me) you've had enough of flowery books about mindfulness, you'll love the practical, playful, 'no-BS' approach of this one. It's an excellent self-help book in and of itself, but also a very useful adjunct to working with a therapist. Read it, enjoy it, apply it, and reap the rewards."

—**Russ Harris**, author of the million-copy best-seller, *The Happiness Trap*

"If you don't believe that life is merely a race where you speed around accomplishing the most goals possible—but that it is about accomplishing them in a meaning, purposeful, and satisfying way—then this book is for you! While most books either tell you why or how to change, *Finding Your Why and Finding Your Way* gives you a simple yet chock-full-of-effective-strategies approach to addressing both. This book will supercharge your ability to live a successful and balanced life, where you focus deeply on what matters most to you. As someone who truly values getting at the *why* of change as deeply as possible, I could not recommend this book more highly."

—**Michael V. Pantalon, PhD**, author of *Instant Influence*

"*Finding Your Why and Finding Your Way* will increase clarity and endurance on the journey that is your life. No matter where you are on your personal journey, this readable guide will help you identify what matters to you, sustain motivation and commitment, and identify and overcome obstacles while increasing psychological flexibility."

—**Patricia Bach, PhD**, ACT therapist and trainer,
and coauthor of *ACT in Practice* and *Committed Action in Practice*

"Filled with personal examples and relatable stories of others, *Finding Your Why and Finding Your Way* paves a fantastic path to empowered goal setting and living mindfully according to what matters most. For anyone who has ever wanted clarity of action in the service of achievement, success, and healthy living, this self-help journey is for you. Read, work, grow, and thrive with this excellent book on finding your way!"

—**Robyn D. Walser, PhD**, licensed clinical psychologist; author of *The Heart of ACT*;
and coauthor of *Learning ACT*, *The Mindful Couple*, *Acceptance and Commitment Therapy
for the Treatment of Post-Traumatic Stress Disorder and Trauma-Related Problems*, and
The ACT Workbook for Anger

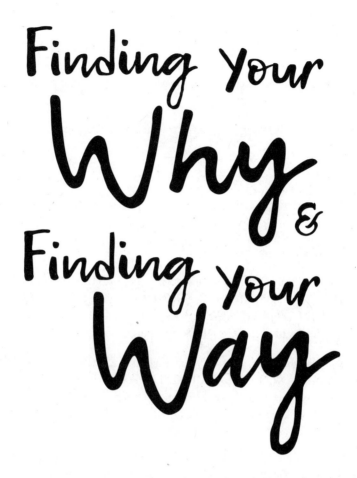

Finding Your Why & Finding Your Way

An Acceptance & Commitment Therapy Workbook to Help You Identify What You Care About & Reach Your Goals

DANIEL J. MORAN, PHD, BCBA-D
SIRI MING, PHD, BCBA-D

New Harbinger Publications, Inc.

Publisher's Note

NEW HARBINGER PUBLICATIONS is a registered trademark of New Harbinger Publications, Inc.

New Harbinger Publications is an employee-owned company.

Copyright © 2023 by Daniel J. Moran and Siri Ming
New Harbinger Publications, Inc.
5674 Shattuck Avenue
Oakland, CA 94609
www.newharbinger.com

The activity "Am I Living in Line with My Values" from UNDERSTANDING AND APPLYING RELATIONAL FRAME THEORY: MASTERING THE FOUNDATIONS OF COMPLEX LANGUAGE IN OUR WORK AND LIVES AS BEHAVIOR ANALYSTS by Siri Ming, Julia Fiebig, and Evelyn Gould, copyright © 2023 by Siri Ming, Julia Fiebig, and Evelyn Gould. Used by permission of New Harbinger Publications.

The exercise "Examining the Fiber of Your Being" is adapted from LEARNING ACT FOR GROUP TREATMENT: AN ACCEPTANCE AND COMMITMENT THERAPY SKILLS TRAINING MANUAL FOR THERAPISTS by Darrah Westrup and Joann Wright, copyright © 2017 by Darrah Westrup and Joann Wright. Used by permission of New Harbinger Publications.

Cover design by Sara Christian; Acquired by Catharine Meyers; Edited by Jean Blomquist

---

Library of Congress Cataloging-in-Publication Data on file

Printed in the United States of America

25   24   23

10   9   8   7   6   5   4   3   2   1

First Printing

Contents

Part One
Planning Your Journey with the MAP

Chapter 1   Orienting with the MAP   3

Chapter 2   Unfolding the MAP   17

Part Two
Finding Your Why

Chapter 3   You Are Here   33

Chapter 4   What I Care About   53

Part Three
Finding Your Way

Chapter 5   Doing   73

Chapter 6   Here Now   95

Chapter 7   Accepting   107

Chapter 8   Noticing   127

Chapter 9   I Am   141

Chapter 10   The MAP: A Global View   155

References   165

Part One

Planning Your Journey with the MAP

CHAPTER 1

Orienting with the MAP

Take a moment to pay attention to what you're experiencing here and now. What can you see and hear around you? Investigate a bit further: *Why* are you doing what you're doing right here, right now? Thousands of small choices brought you to reading this page at this moment. How do you feel about those choices? Are you feeling lost in life? Or maybe things are ticking along for you, but you're still looking for some direction. Or maybe you've found your peak spot and want to grow from this strong foundation.

Wherever you stand, you won't be standing still for long. Everyone's journey continues until their final day, and finding your why and finding your way on this expedition makes it all valuable and worthwhile. *Finding your why* refers to the ongoing search for what brings meaning and purpose to your activities in different areas of life, discovering the qualities and actions that most reflect your values, or how you want to act and who you want to be. *Finding your way* relates to discovering and committing to actions that bring you closer to fulfilling your purpose, and that skillfully bring you back to that valued path when you get distracted or stuck.

This book's central tool—the Mindful Action Plan (MAP)—can help you reorient yourself in life's terrain. The MAP can help you find your why and find your way through life with deliberate, mindful, purposeful action.

Life is a journey, as the saying goes, but we rarely take the time to map it out. A map helps you find your way home to safety and comfort, and can also guide you toward favorable new destinations when you already know where you stand. Maps can reorient you if you feel lost, and guide you step-by-step in valuable directions. Ultimately, the MAP will help you explore the territory of who you are, where you could go, and how you'll travel.

We invite you to return to these critical questions as you begin your journey, and as you travel your path: Why? Where are you heading, and why would you need a MAP? What would it mean to follow your chosen path, and how would it look to live your life fully with intention and purpose? Each of us has a unique answer. But generally, in guiding people to use the MAP, we've found that we're confident in our journey's direction when we feel truly present in the moment, are able to *be here now*, and are focusing on the activity at hand while finding meaning simply by doing it. And we also feel sure of our direction when we know our action serves a meaningful purpose—when we're doing something that has a larger importance and value in our lives. We are even more certain we're following the right path when we can stay dedicated to it even when our minds tell us that we might fail or be terribly hurt along the way. The journey has meaning when we look around us and still take the next step, even when it feels risky, because we know we're guided by what's important to us, and we can do something to serve those deep, core values we have here and now.

As the saying goes, a journey of a thousand miles begins with a single step. Making a journey worthwhile requires finding your why and finding your way. Why are you choosing to move in certain directions, and how are you going to take those steps, especially when obstacles appear? Only you can determine where you want to go, and this book helps you figure that out, envision your path clearly, and create a MAP for going toward personally important directions. The Mindful Action Plan focuses on taking that first step, and then the next, and the next—and making sure you can keep your sights on where you're going as well as appreciating where you are now. It invites you to be here now, accepting your feelings, noticing your thoughts, while doing what you care about. It focuses on helping you take mindful action.

What Is Mindful Action?

Mindful action is purposeful, present-focused, committed behavior while maximally attending to what you choose to make important while unhindered by distractions. We understand we're throwing some nerdy applied behavioral science terms at you right off the bat, but bear with us as we aim to communicate the concept of mindful action in an understandable manner while also staying true to the science of human behavior. After all, the Mindful Action Plan is built on an evidence-based psychological approach known as acceptance and commitment therapy (Hayes, Strosahl, and Wilson 2012). Before we get to the explanation of acceptance and commitment therapy (ACT) and how it applies to the MAP, let's carefully unpack the definition of mindful action.

Mindful Action Is Purposeful

Being purposeful is one of the main aims of the MAP. *Merriam-Webster* defines "purposeful" two ways:

1. fully committed to achieving a goal

2. made, given, or done with full awareness of what one is doing

Mindful action is *fully committed to achieving a goal*, and done with *full awareness of what one is doing*. Throughout this book, we'll highlight how to build skills not only for executing goal-oriented behaviors but also for creating habits that are directed by what you value, and for keeping your awareness sharp while doing so. If you look up the word "why" in the *Merriam-Webster* dictionary, you'll see that it means "for what…purpose." In other words, when you're finding your why, you're finding the reason to be purposeful.

Mindful Action Is Present-Focused

Now is the only time you can engage in goal-oriented behaviors and value-directed habits. You cannot behave tomorrow, nor can you behave yesterday. You can't behave in five minutes or five minutes ago. *Now* is the only time action happens. This is why we strongly encourage meditation practices, even as secular behavioral scientists who have no agenda for changing your spiritual or religious beliefs. Practicing the skills that meditation teaches—like the ability to encounter your own experience as it is in the moment, without judgment—aids you to *be more reliably in the here and now*, meaning you'll be focused on your actions and the world around you. If you want to have a life well lived, then becoming more aware of what you're doing in the present moment plays a role in that endeavor. If signals from the world cue you to do a valued action here and now, but you're too busy thinking about other things there and then, you won't embrace life's opportunities as impactfully as you could. Practicing mindful action can positively influence your ability to stay present-focused so you don't miss vital opportunities.

Metaphorically speaking, sometimes we're like a person listening to the radio while wearing headphones. At times, we hear the deejay playing an uninteresting, crummy song recorded in the past, and other times, the deejay is advertising something going on far away and in the future. While wearing these headphones, we're awash in sounds from the radio about there and then that distract us from focusing on what's happening here and now. Unfortunately, the headphones also prevent us from hearing when the world whispers, "Hey, here's a real opportunity for you to have the life you want to lead right now!" Instead, we only hear loud, repetitive ditties from the past or advertisements that lure us into the future, and we miss the precious possibility. How often have you missed those whispers? How many more subtle cues will go unheard while you remain stuck thinking about the past or the future and missing great opportunities to live your life well? The Mindful Action Plan helps you remove those headphones, listen more carefully to your vibrant environment, and generate motivation to take advantage of every valuable opportunity.

Mindful Action Involves Committed Behavior

Getting where you want to go requires taking overt, measurable steps. It involves committed action. A commitment is *action in the direction of what you care about even in the presence of obstacles.* Since one of the aims of this book is to help you learn how to keep your commitments, let's dissect that definition:

"action"—As you can see in the first word of our definition, committing requires acting. When it comes to living a life of purpose and vitality, many people *say* they're committed to certain things, but they often don't *act* that way. Just talking about doing something is not committing. You must identify behaviors leading to a life of purpose and vitality, and then choose to take those actions. We'll help you identify those behaviors in chapter 5.

"in the direction of what you care about"—This suggests commitments are personal and based on your values. When you find your *why* for making the commitment, clarifying your reason for caring about the processes and outcomes of your effort that link your actions to the things you value, you're more likely to maintain those commitments over the long term. We'll explore your values in chapters 3 and 4.

"even in the presence of obstacles"—This reminds us that accomplishing important tasks is not simple or easy. Your chance for success is increased by devising a plan for dealing with complications, because hurdles will inevitably arise. Committed behavior does not stop when difficulties occur—acknowledging that there are stumbling blocks, and working to solve them, is one of the hallmarks of committed action. The later chapters in this book will address how to move forward when your personal obstacles stop you in your tracks, and we'll give you tools to deal with various hindrances—such as fear, anger, self-doubt, procrastination, anxiety, boredom, and more—that might impede your commitment.

Mindful Action Involves Maximally Attending to What You Choose to Make Important

The Mindful Action Plan can be about anything you want. Your aims for personal growth are related to what you value, and we can't tell you what you should choose to make important. We've seen the MAP be useful for doing many important things like starting an art career, raising a troubled child, starting a business, raising money for charity by running distance races, improving relationships, recovering from addiction, and becoming healthier. The MAP can help you with your own personal-growth goals. Alternatively, the MAP can also support you to take that gut-wrenching step upward from the abyss, forward from your paralyzing fear, or toward a place of well-deserved health and self-kindness. This journey shall be what *you* choose to make important.

We also want to highlight what we mean by the nerdy phrase "maximally attend to" in the heading above. Mindful action is about effectively focusing—for as long as it takes—on successfully completing your present goals while expressing your life-long values. In other words, mindful action is about *focusing most of your attention on what you choose to be important in your life*, and the MAP aims to help you do that successfully. Mindful action comes from paying attention to what is going on here and now, and staying true to your values.

Mindful Action Is Unhindered by Distractions

In the twenty-first century, distractions bombard us constantly. Every day we aim to focus on something important in our life, but distractions throw us off our path. We're enticed by social media, called to pay attention to society's expectations, and influenced to juggle in the carnival of multitasking. The world around us grabs our time and efforts, and it saps energy and impedes us from doing what we care about. However, these external interferences don't have to inhibit us from doing what we value, as long as we mindfully refocus on what's important to us.

But it's not just the external world that distracts us. We distract ourselves. Our internal world of moods, emotions, urges, and thoughts also draws us away from our chosen path. The MAP helps you become unhindered from disruptive feelings and thoughts. We strategically described mindful action as "unhindered." While this book is science-based and secular, we also embrace the practical wisdom from spiritual traditions thousands of years old. Zen Buddhism teaches about the "five hindrances" that can have a negative impact on a life well lived: anger, laziness, doubt, sensory desire, and restlessness. Other spiritual traditions similarly identify obstacles along the path to living a meaningful or virtuous life: Catholicism's seven deadly sins include lust, greed, envy, pride, sloth, wrath, and gluttony. Sufism describes stumbling blocks on the path that include desire, anger, anxiety, and boredom.

And Western psychological traditions have identified many concerns that have a negative influence on well-being—fear, anxiety, stress, depression, resentment, bitterness, compulsivity, and many more. According to these traditions, the *obstacles within the human condition* can be addressed by creating *a context supporting the practice of mindfulness*.

Why Mindful *Action*?

We didn't use the term "mindfulness" in this book until the end of the last paragraph—and our focus on mindful *action* over mindfulness is deliberate. Mindfulness has been defined in many ways by scientists, meditators, and spiritual leaders, and that's where the problem lies. There are so many different definitions that, while respectfully embracing and integrating what was said by others, we as behavioral scientists want to start from scratch and establish a viewpoint for what mindfulness can be objectively shown to do for you—namely, helping you engage in observable mindful action.

We have a great deal of respect for mindfulness, engage in mindfulness exercises ourselves, and love that ancient mindfulness practices are influencing people today to have a life well lived. Our reluctance to use the term "mindfulness" in the book until now is because we're trying to highlight something a bit different. We want you to see the difference between mindful action and mindfulness so that you observe a measurable impact on your valued living from this book. One problem with mindful*ness* is that the suffix "-ness" creates an abstract noun representing a quality. As behavior scientists who are trying to help people, we don't want to just study *abstract* things denoting *quality*. We want to look at *concrete* results that can be *quantified* through measuring behavior change. We're interested in mindful actions. It's a subtle difference, but an important one. If you incorporate mindfulness into your life, how would you know its impact? People who have incorporated mindfulness into their lives talk about how they are *doing* more productive and less unhealthy actions. Ultimately, mindfulness can lead to behavior change—including the behavior of relating to how we think and feel—so this book goes right to the solid, measurable topic: how to engage in mindful action.

The MAP creates a context supporting mindfulness practices, and throughout the book, we'll refer to mindfulness practices and mindfulness exercises. These are actions you might already be doing, like meditating, fasting, or praying. Your own usual way of mindfulness is encouraged—what's already out there in the mindfulness world is worthy and helpful, so we're not asking anyone to change their approach. And if you don't have a mindfulness practice, you'll be invited to consider how it could be practical and helpful to you, and to begin to incorporate the exercises into your life. However, we won't dogmatically demand disciplined, rigorous meditation practice, but rather we'll gently encourage a flexible way through which you can build several psychological skills to deal with various hindrances to mindful action. The MAP encourages learning to simply notice and detach from unhelpful thoughts, while also learning how to accept difficult feelings. We'll unpack the practical usefulness of mindfulness practices by teaching how to deal with personal obstacles while committing to valuable goals.

So, putting it all back together, mindful action is purposeful, present-focused, committed behavior that you do while maximally attending to what you choose to make important, and unhindered by distractions. More specifically, mindful action is:

- *fully committed to achieving a goal,*
- done with *full awareness of what one is doing*
- while aiming to *be more reliably in the here and now,* and
- engaged in *action in the direction of what you care about*
- by *focusing most of your attention on what you choose to be important in your life,*
- not stopped by *obstacles within the human condition*
- by building psychological skills through *a context supporting the practice of mindfulness.*

If this sounds like a direction you'd like to take in your life, the MAP is your guide for the journey.

Mindful Action Builds Psychological Flexibility

Using the MAP will build up your psychological flexibility, which is a human characteristic strongly related to other healthy attributes, skills, and outcomes. "Psychological flexibility describes the capacity to contact the present moment while also being aware of thoughts and emotions—without trying to change those private experiences or be controlled by them—and depending upon the situation, persisting in or changing behavior in the pursuit of values and goals" (Moran 2015). Comparing the definition for psychological flexibility with our definition for mindful action, you can see that mindful action is an overt display of psychological flexibility. Mindful action is psychological flexibility made obvious. When you're contacting the present moment, have a healthy relationship with your thoughts and emotions, embrace your current circumstances, and demonstrate a willingness to behave effectively in pursuing your values (which is psychological flexibility), you're demonstrating purposeful, present-focused, committed behavior while maximally attending to what you choose to make important, and unhindered by distractions (which is mindful action).

Research demonstrates that improvements in psychological flexibility are related to improvements in many mental health conditions (A-Tjak et al. 2015), including depression (Dindo et al. 2021; Shirazipour 2022), substance abuse (Ii et al. 2019), and anxiety (Kelson et al. 2019). Increasing psychological flexibility is also beneficial for improving performance and well-being in many areas of life while reducing the impact of stress and burnout. Broadly speaking, people with higher psychological flexibility demonstrate improved quality of life, increased adaptive functioning, and a greater commitment to their values with a diminished susceptibility to distracting thoughts and troublesome emotions (Ciarrochi, Bilich, and Godsell 2010). Speaking more specifically, research shows that work, education, relationships, personal growth, and leisure activities are effectively improved with higher psychological flexibility.

- **Work:** Higher psychological flexibility is related to more productivity and effectiveness, accelerated leadership skills, an increased propensity to innovate, improved financial literacy, and making fewer errors in job tasks (Flaxman, Bond, and Livheim 2013; Moran 2015).

- **Education:** Academic achievement and other important school-based measures are improved with interventions that increase psychological flexibility (Paliliunas, Belisle, and Dixon 2018; Perkins et al. 2021; Piri, Hosseininasab, and Livarjani 2020).

- **Relationships:** Higher psychological flexibility has been shown to strengthen interpersonal relationships among children, teens, and adults, along with parenting relationships (Azimifar et al. 2016; Cho 2013; Rosales-Villacrés et al. 2021; Amini Naghani et al. 2020).

- **Personal growth and health:** Self-improvement is an area of the human experience where psychological flexibility really shines. Mental health issues, such as depression, anxiety, stress, and anger, are appropriately diminished with improvements in psychological flexibility. Higher psychological flexibility is also related to healthy management of weight, cancer, diabetes, chronic pain, smoking cessation, and many other medical issues (Lillis et al. 2021; Faryabi et al. 2021; Saeidi et al. 2021; Yadavari, Naderi, and Makvandi 2021; Bricker et al. 2022; Rose et al. 2022).

- **Leisure:** The activities we do for fun, personal accomplishment, excitement, and relaxation are also influenced by psychological flexibility. It has been shown to relate to playing individual sports and team sports more effectively, improving chess playing skills, and having positive effects on hobbies and exercise (Lundgren et al. 2021; Bu et al. 2020; Ruiz and Luciano 2012; Ivanova et al. 2016; Kangasniemi et al. 2015; Swain and Bodkin-Allen 2017).

Through this book, you'll see the unique benefits that psychological flexibility and mindful action can have for you.

Acceptance and Commitment Therapy and the MAP

Research on psychological flexibility—and the basic cartography of the MAP—comes from the science of acceptance and commitment therapy (ACT), an effective, evidence-based psychological approach. The ACT community has a vision for "the alleviation of human suffering and the advancement of human well-being through research and practice" (Association for Contextual Behavioral Science 2022). For decades, this vibrant community of ACT scholars and practitioners has been helping vast numbers of people. In addition, Acceptance and Commitment Training (ACTraining; see Moran 2015) applies similar principles and applications to other challenges, such as leadership, productivity, and athletic endeavors. Over 900 scientific studies show how ACT and ACTraining move the needle on important measures in a wide array of human struggles.

The Mindful Action Plan simplifies acceptance and commitment therapy and ACTraining so you can custom-fit the applications to your own life challenges, helping you use ACT principles and build skills for accepting your own emotions while committing to the important directions you choose to take with your life. We'll look next at how the traditional ACT model outlines its six components and translate them into the user-friendly application of the Mindful Action Plan.

Introducing the ACT Hexagon

ACT integrates six components, known as the ACT Hexagon, to help increase psychological flexibility: perspective taking, contacting the present moment, accepting, defusing, committed action, and valuing. Each one involves skills building, and they all have mutual relationships with each other, so when you improve one skill, other skills are promoted. In part two of this book, we'll visit each ACT component from the viewpoint of the Mindful Action Plan, and experiment with incorporating ACT into your daily life. We'll spend the rest of the workbook discussing these skills and how you can tailor-make MAPs for mindful action during your journey. Let's look now at the six components on the ACT Hexagon, and note briefly how they're related to the MAP.

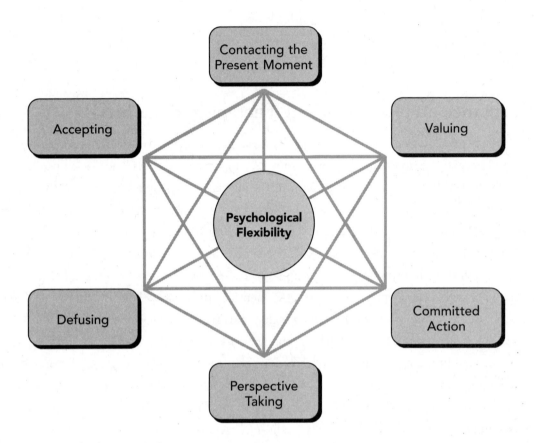

Perspective Taking. ACT helps you develop a steadfast sense of self. You can take a perspective on the world around you that no one else has. You can take a breath at any moment, observe this ever-changing world in which we live, and also contact something unshakeable, unchangeable, and unwavering: you! You are at the center of every single experience. Your core "self" is available to you whenever you need it and wherever you are. Whether facing challenges or enjoying celebrations, there is a center of that experience: you! ACT helps you learn to view your existence as unencumbered by how you talk about yourself, the roles you assume, and the memories and anxieties that weigh you down. You become aware of your core self, and realize that—as long as you live—nothing around you can stop you from saying the powerful phrase "I am."

In the Mindful Action Plan, you'll be asked to come in contact with the *I am* experience, develop it, and leverage it when the world around you changes. Perspective taking in ACT is the skill of contacting the experience of I Am on the MAP. We'll explore this section of the MAP further in chapter 9.

Contacting the Present Moment. ACT utilizes a mindfulness-based approach to behavior change. Decades of research and centuries of tradition suggest that the mindfulness practice of centering yourself in the here and now can have an impactful influence on well-being. ACT proposes that mindfulness practice helps you have a life well lived, and the MAP focuses on building mindfulness skills and creating a habit of mindful action.

With the MAP, you're invited to utilize mindfulness exercises——both with deliberate practice and also at unplanned times—to integrate yourself with the here and now. Contacting the present moment is the skill of being in the Here Now on the MAP. We'll explore this section of the MAP further in chapter 6.

Accepting. We're taught early in life to control our feelings and avoid negative emotions. In the short term, that seems like helpful advice, but it can become an issue when people engage in problematic actions to avoid feeling nervous, sad, frustrated, and the like. As uncomfortable as those feelings may be, they're part of the human condition and inherent in a life well lived. ACT teaches you to be willing to have the natural feelings that show up as you engage in vital, meaningful action.

With the Mindful Action Plan, you exercise the skill of accepting your emotions, sensations, urges, and other ways you feel internally. Accepting is the term used in ACT and also on the MAP. We'll explore this section of the MAP further in chapter 7.

Defusing. What you think about the world around you and your actions in it, and how you relate to those thoughts, has a significant impact on your journey. ACT promotes the skill of unfastening yourself and your actions from unhelpful thoughts, and developing a fresher viewpoint on the language that happens between your ears and behind your eyes. Your mind gives you lots of thoughts throughout the day, and ACT encourages you to simply notice those thoughts, if they're unhelpful, rather than getting attached to them. Instead of being stuck to—or "fusing" to—the thoughts we think, ACT encourages defusing from those thoughts.

With the Mindful Action Plan, you'll learn to detach your actions from your thoughts. In ACT, this is called "defusing," and we call it Noticing on the MAP. We'll explore this section of the MAP further in chapter 8.

Committed Action. You're behaving all the time. Sometimes you're doing things reflexively, habitually, mindlessly, and—hopefully, at other times—purposefully. You're engaged in some kind of action all day long, and ACT aims to accelerate how often you're engaged in committed action, instead of just going on autopilot. The name of the approach specifies "commitment," indicating a focus on dedicating time and efforts to *doing* meaningful things. In fact, that's the term used in the Mindful

Action Plan: you clarify what actions you'll be doing on the MAP. Committed Action in ACT is Doing on the MAP.

Valuing. Committed actions happen more frequently when there's a reason *why* you're doing them. One of the major purposes of this workbook is finding your "why," and ACT spends time encouraging people to clarify what they value in life to motivate further action. Valuing is something you do: you actively care about some things in your life, and you're ambivalent about other things. In ACT, you're given the opportunity to explore the reasons for the actions you find yourself doing, and why some behaviors seem more meaningful, vital, and valuable. You start to author your "why," not in terms of some existential purpose for your being, but rather as the purpose for your actions.

In the Mindful Action Plan, you leverage your ability to use language to declare for yourself what you care about. Valuing describes what personally and meaningfully motivates our actions in ACT, and is What I Care About on the MAP. We'll explore this section of the MAP further in chapter 4.

We've just reviewed the components on the ACT hexagon model. Now take a look at how the Mindful Action Plan reinterprets those skills:

I am here now,

accepting the way I feel, noticing my thoughts,

while doing what I care about.

Embracing this powerful statement could significantly improve the way you live. Imagine that you could maintain this viewpoint throughout your day, throughout your difficult times, throughout your life! In this workbook, you'll get better at each of these areas, improving your psychological flexibility, which in turn will increase your abilities to act on the meaningful elements of your life. As we go through each area of the MAP in part two, we will share stories of people using the MAP for a variety of purposes. These stories will give you examples of how you might customize your own MAP statements and how the MAP can be used in lots of different ways. As a tool for psychological flexibility, we encourage you to use the MAP flexibly!

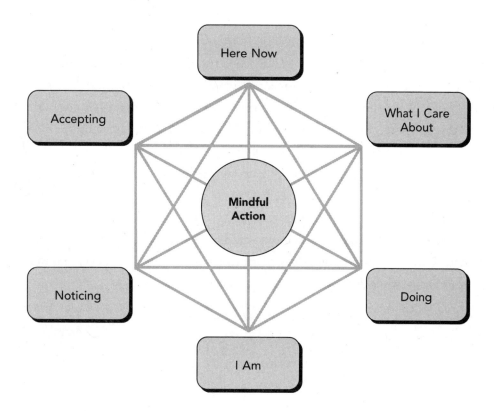

The MAP Checklist

The Mindful Action Plan summarizes the crucial components of ACT in a checklist format, allowing you to organize your efforts, stay accountable to the contributing factors of mindfulness, and maintain consistency with the whole process. Checklists are a very powerful way to stay on course toward your desired goals. We highly recommend that you download the MAP and print it out to use regularly as a checklist to help you stay on track. (Visit http://www.newharbinger.com/50713 to download the MAP and other helpful materials. See the very back of this book for details.) We highly recommend acquiring a few clipboards for your MAPs, and keeping them in places where you'd like to accelerate your mindful actions. The MAP will help you learn and integrate the six ACT components to promote psychological flexibility—that is, you'll learn skill sets for mindful action. In this way, the MAP helps you find your why and find your way on this journey of life, and this workbook will be your field guide.

Moving Forward

In this chapter, you were introduced to mindful action, psychological flexibility, and the theoretical basis for this book, acceptance and commitment therapy. You also considered the basic question that informs this book: *Why* are you doing what you're doing, right here and right now? An important corollary to this question is this: Is there something you could be doing differently or better, to really make your journey through life a mindful, purposeful, and fulfilling one?

These are big questions. And in this workbook, we'll help you find answers to them. In the next chapter, we'll unfold the MAP so you can see how to use it to get where you want to be, and then in chapter 3, you'll have a chance to figure out where you are right now. After that, you'll grow the skills to take stronger and sturdier strides in your chosen directions and build the skills of psychological flexibility with fluent mindful action. You'll learn to say: I am here now, accepting the way I feel, noticing my thoughts, while doing what I care about. Let's begin.

CHAPTER 2

Unfolding the MAP

As you unfold the MAP (Mindful Action Plan), you'll discover that this tool guides you on your journey and helps you reach the destination you desire. It helps you to both travel your true path and prepare yourself for a values-based, skillful commitment to your *why* and your *way*. Because the best way to become familiar with a new tool is to use it, let's learn to do just that.

THE MINDFUL ACTION PLAN

I am here now,
accepting the way I feel and noticing my thoughts,
while doing what I care about.

Date: _____

	Addressing Internal-World Issues	✓
I Am	Observe if you are being influenced by any unhelpful self-descriptions. Let go of any problematic thoughts you are believing about your self.	
Here Now	Center your situational awareness on what you are doing. Contact what is happening here and now. Rather than getting wrapped up in events not in your present control, let go of these distracting events. Focus on what is relevant to your actions.	
Accepting	Allow yourself to acknowledge any emotions you are having without trying to control the emotions. Be willing to simply have those feelings while moving forward with valuable actions.	
Noticing	Observe thoughts that arise while moving forward with valued actions. Let those thoughts go if they are not helpful. Treat distracting thoughts as disconnected from action while choosing to act in a meaningful manner.	

	To-Do List		
Doing			

	Values-Based Motivation	
What I Care About	Personal Values: Describe your motivation for engaging in your chosen actions and why you aim for optimal performance.	

Designing Success with Performance Management	
Make sure all required resources for successful actions have been acquired.	
Publicly announce your commitment to meet performance goals.	
Alert your accountability partner about your commitment and goals.	
Describe incentives, performance criteria, and deadlines:	

Working the MAP

At the top of the MAP, you'll see a sentence that exemplifies psychological flexibility: "I am here now, accepting the way I feel, noticing my thoughts, while doing what I care about." Being able to resonate with that statement will help support your success, no matter where you're going with the MAP—whether your journey relates to your work or education, connecting more deeply in your relationships, continuing to grow personally, maintaining or improving your health, reconnecting to leisure activities that bring you joy, or any other vital goals in your life that serve what you most value and aspire to do and be. Note the checklist on the right side of the MAP. Using checklists to improve performance helps people stay committed and ensures that they engage in all the necessary actions for task completion (Gawande 2009). You'll use the MAP checklist to build your psychological flexibility step-by-step. It may seem ironic to use something as rigid as a checklist to build flexibility, but the checklist helps you break down complex skills into their components, practice them until you can do them very well, and then combine them all together. If you wanted to learn the complex skill of playing jazz piano, for instance, you'd start by learning the major and minor scales, and then build from there. If you want to be psychologically flexible, you start by focusing on the major components and the minor details of engaging in mindful action. You'll use the MAP to go through the skills you need to execute your tasks. It will also serve as a to-do list to ensure you stay on track with your committed activities. Each checkbox is an invitation to check in with yourself and check off that the response was completed.

In this chapter, we'll go over all six components of the MAP, and then we'll spend a chapter on each as we move forward with the book. But we'll have an odd starting point. Rather than beginning at the top of the MAP, as you might with a typical worksheet, we're going to start almost at the bottom. This may seem a bit strange, given that the MAP is our guiding document, but as the influential performance consultant Stephen Covey was fond of saying, we want to "begin with the end in mind." Specifically, you're going to begin with the What I Care About section. (Note: The components that appear in the left column of the MAP will be capitalized in the text when they refer specifically to the MAP.)

What I Care About

What I Care About	Values-Based Motivation	
	Personal Values: Describe your motivation for engaging in your chosen actions and why you aim for optimal performance.	

This is where you start taking practical steps with finding your why and finding your way. In asking you to describe your personal values as well as to describe "your motivation for engaging in your chosen actions and why you aim for optimal performance," the MAP invites you to explore—and then clarify—what you choose to be meaningful. Reflecting on this before you start doing things can be truly revolutionary. The MAP encourages you to engage in mindful actions that are fundamentally *purposeful*, so starting with What I Care About will help you identify your purpose and clarify *why* you're choosing to go the *way* you're going to go.

We invite you to explore the unique, individual purposes of your life from your own perspective, and how your choices for action—moment by moment, day after day—can be linked to what you find personally meaningful. These are your values. *Values* are what you care about doing and the way you choose to do those actions. Parenting your child, leading your work team, contributing to your local community are values, and you can also value doing these actions lovingly, effectively, and generously. Values are ways of talking about what we want our life to be about. While creating your MAPs, you'll want to write what you genuinely find meaningful about the actions you'll take for the particular time frame you're focusing on. These declarations will guide you to a path and describe how you'll walk that path.

A Quick Survey of Values

What do you care about? What's truly important to you? What do you want your life to be about? Use these questions to prime the pump, then do some brainstorming and record at least a few ideas that come to mind immediately about what you really care about.

_____

_____

_____

_____

_____

At this point, your MAP is a blank canvas. We built the MAP framework for planning the actions you'll take and strengthening the skills you'll need for your particular journey. We can't plan your journey for you or tell you why you'd want to take any particular path. This workbook is designed for you to clarify your values for yourself so you can plan the life journey *you* want to take—your psychologically flexible path to a life well lived. On a psychologically flexible journey, you'll often check in with yourself to see if you're heading in a meaningful direction—one that you care about—and then you'll take steps toward doing mindful actions.

Doing

Now we're moving to the middle of the MAP: the To-Do List. Here, you'll find space to write up to ten different committed actions. The Doing section is where you'll start planning committed behaviors and finding your way, and we limit it to just ten to help you stay focused. We highly recommend writing out your to-do list on a MAP rather than on a sticky note or the back of an old envelope so that you have an actual plan for how and why you'll execute what you're doing. This list can range from simply setting the alarm clock before you go to bed to calling your lawyer to incorporate a start-up company in the morning. What you'll be doing is entirely your choice, and this book can't tell you what to do, but it can give you some tips for finding the answer.

In the Doing section of the MAP, you're invited to write measurable actions that bring your life in line with the values you wrote as What I Care About. In other words, it's the *action* part of the Mindful Action Plan: doing what is vital and purposeful in your life by keeping your commitments. Use this as your to-do list for organizing steps you'll take in your journey.

Doing	To-Do List			

Be aware that mindful action is significantly more than simply completing your to-do list. We're talking about doing things on your to-do list to simply point out that having a life well lived, in a psychologically flexible manner, will come down to the particular daily behaviors that comprise your lifestyle. One major benefit of using the MAP is that it helps you contact meaning in your day-in-day-out behaviors as you stay committed to executing these actions well.

You'll notice that there is another part of the MAP beyond the six components, and it's an annex to the Doing section. The Mindful Action Plan also utilizes the powerful techniques of performance management to support success in doing what you care about. Notice that the MAP has a built-in reward structure. The Designing Success with Performance Management section provides an opportunity to plan how to accomplish your tasks and how to incentivize your behavior. Leveraging positive reinforcement to provide consequences for mindful action will increase commitment to the values-based behaviors you'll be doing.

Designing Success with Performance Management	
Make sure all required resources for successful actions have been acquired.	
Publicly announce your commitment to meet performance goals.	
Alert your accountability partner about your commitment and goals.	
Describe incentives, performance criteria, and deadlines:	

Brainstorming What You'll Be Doing

It's important to be quite specific every time you use the MAP, and we invite you to start brainstorming now. In the last exercise, you were asked, What do you care about? Now, write how you will engage in actions related to those values. What will you be doing?

_____

_____

_____

_____

_____

Recall that the Doing section of the MAP is related to committed action in the ACT model, and that a commitment is _action in the direction of what you care about even in the presence of obstacles._ So far, we've talked about engaging in action in the direction of what you care about, and now we'll talk about how to deal with the presence of obstacles to the action you might take with the four other components on the MAP: the sections labeled I Am, Here Now, Accepting, and Noticing. These sections help you stay on your path and return when you've lost your way.

I Am

Take a moment to consider this:

You are.

That's it.

You exist.

When you tell this to yourself, then you'll say something like "I am." This may seem silly and trite, but truly let this message resonate: _you exist._ You've been _you_ your whole life. There's never been anyone like you, and you'll never be anyone else. You look at the world from a unique, specific viewpoint. That "self," or "perspective," or "point of view," is an unbroken, steadfast, and strong entity, and no matter what has ever happened to you, no matter what does happen to you, as long as you're alive, you experience that "self." Whatever you're in the middle of, you can take a moment (and even a breath) and say to yourself, *I am*. This grounds and liberates you. Realize "I am" is a full sentence, and it will always be true as long as you're alive.

All other statements about yourself after "I am…" only sprinkle more definitions onto this core essence—ones that may or may not be true or helpful, and ones that may or may not last. You might end up saying things like "I am a good person," "I am lost," "I am funny." For most of us, the labels we use for ourselves are sometimes helpful and sometimes unhelpful. While journeying, we quite often carry a backpack filled with self-blame, insults, and other uncomfortable labels. Truly learning the skill of focusing on "I am" when needed will lighten the load and help you on your journey.

| I Am | Observe if you are being influenced by any unhelpful self-descriptions. Let go of any problematic thoughts you are believing about your self. | |

Recall that in ACT, this kind of flexibility is called *perspective taking*. Perspective taking allows us to see that while we might describe ourselves in particular ways—a parent, a student, a survivor, a failure, a worrier, a warrior, a procrastinator, efficient, skilled, tired, excited, or a thousand other nouns and adjectives—these labels may be parts of who we are, but they don't define us. As Walt Whitman wrote, "I am large, I contain multitudes." Perspective taking lets us take a birds-eye view of our "self" and see that a continuous thread, a core sense of self, weaves through all our experiences. It helps us to move away from the specific labels we so often use and to embrace the perspective of this core sense of self, with an ability to observe the environment and our interactions in it with nonjudgment and a degree of objectivity.

Checking In with Your Self

Take a moment now to consider how you think about yourself. What are your stories of who you are? If you were to describe yourself to others, what would you say? How do your stories either make your load a bit easier to carry or weigh you down? Make some notes about this, becoming aware of your own perspective on who you are and preparing to let some of these stories go on the journey ahead.

_____

_____

_____

_____

_____

Here Now

Being in the here and now is the only place and time we can be. A critically important point of the Mindful Action Plan is that the only time you can behave is now. The only place you can behave is here. But we've all experienced our thoughts, sensations, urges, and emotions taking us out of the here and now and putting us in the there and then. There's nothing wrong with planning for the future or reminiscing about the past. However, it's harder to be psychologically flexible when we worry about the future and ruminate about the past. During our journey, if we're wrapped up in worries about tomorrows or traumas from our yesterdays, we might miss signposts for values-based actions in the present moment. Being present-focused is crucial for mindful action.

Mindfulness practices often suggest that you build a skill of contacting the present moment by *maximally attending to* your breathing, and being *unhindered* by distractions from that chosen behavior. These distractions can be internal (such as thoughts, feelings, and so on) or external (such as events in your environment). A major theme of this book is to be intensely practical about mindfulness and to embrace the effects such practices have on acting in ways you care about. We urge you to practice mindfulness privately in calm environments and in solitude so you can specifically focus on the skills of being in the here and now. Additionally, we advocate for utilizing these very same skills publicly and overtly when situations are chaotic in the here and now.

This workbook aims to teach you how to bring the attributes of mindfulness to action—especially the action you take in service of your values and goals. Ultimately, you'll find yourself maximally attending to important components to a life well lived outside of your meditations and mindfulness exercises. With practice, rather than getting caught up in distracting events, you'll build a new relationship with them, making it easier to engage in committed actions related to what is truly valuable. The MAP specifically encourages you to tap into those skills while you're doing what you care about. Take a look at another step on the MAP:

| 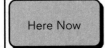 | Center your situational awareness on what you are doing. Contact what is happening here and now. Rather than getting wrapped up in events not in your present control, let go of these distracting events. Focus on what is relevant to your actions. | |

When you practice mindful actions, you learn to center your situational awareness on what you find meaningful. The present moment is the only time you can engage in doing what you care about, so it's helpful to be fluent in the skills that help you stay focused—on items in your to-do list, on the values those items are in service of, and on your experiences of your life as you learn to live it well.

Focusing on the Here Now

When you set out to do the things that you care about, how often do you feel fully present and engaged in the task? What sorts of tasks do you immerse yourself in fully, and what are the settings in which getting things done is easy? How often do thoughts about the past or future distract you? Do you think about the places you've been or alternative destinations you might be going to, instead of taking the next step on your path? What are some thoughts that take you away from your values-based committed actions on a regular basis? What tasks and settings make it difficult to get things done? Keeping tabs on both helpful and distracting elements will increase your awareness of them when you engage in mindful action. List some helpful and distracting elements here.

_____

_____

_____

_____

Accepting

When we talk about accepting, we mean the willingness to genuinely experience feelings without being governed by them. Most of us have not been taught the skill of acceptance, which is crucial for psychological flexibility. In fact, many of us have been taught the opposite—that we should avoid negative emotions and do everything possible to make them go away—for example, "Don't worry, be happy" and "Positive vibes only!" However, it's possible to feel sad, mad, or guilty, and still behave in a values-based manner. Acknowledging your emotions, allowing yourself to embrace the human experience, and willingly feeling these ancient, functional, impactful messages from the core of who you are—*without* reacting to them with aversion or trying to control them—is a key to psychological health.

Resisting, ignoring, and avoiding how you feel leads to some of the most dysfunctional actions you'll ever engage in. The emotions we often resist, ignore, or avoid—such as anger, frustration, discomfort, anxiety, and pain—are actually natural reactions to the human condition. To accept these emotions is to accept your humanity, and accepting your emotions as they naturally arise is the first step to separating what you *feel* from what you *do*. Being skillful at doing that is another element of psychological flexibility, which makes it possible for you to live your life in service of what you value, not just to avoid what you fear. When acting in a psychologically flexible manner, acceptance validates what you're feeling while you're doing what you care about, and it also encourages feeling the feelings fully rather than looking at them as obstacles to overcome. In fact, with the skill of accepting, you might even *harness* these difficult emotions as the fuel for forward motion on your journey with the MAP. Look at how the MAP encourages this kind of uncommon approach for dealing with emotions:

| Accepting | Allow yourself to acknowledge any emotions you are having without trying to control the emotions. Be willing to simply have those feelings while moving forward with valuable actions. | |

A Query About Accepting

Acceptance is a simple concept, but it can be difficult to practice. You can begin by identifying how your own feelings might present a hindrance to mindful action. As you start doing what you care about, do difficult feelings, sensations, or urges slow you down and demand your attention? Write down the emotions that act as obstacles. Would you be able to make some space for them in your backpack on this journey? What healthy actions can you do toward your values and goals in the presence of these emotions?

_____

_____

_____

_____

_____

Noticing

Human beings have been blessed with the skill of language. Sometimes we use words and phrases to communicate with other people via speech, sign language, or text, or we can silently communicate to ourselves with thoughts. When we're fluent with language, we can *describe* events that show up in our lives, *evaluate* if they're good or bad, and *problem solve* for how to get more good and less bad. And then all this "languaging" can have an effect on actually behaving a certain way to solve the problems in our life. The way we connect to language can sway us to make decisive choices. But, thank goodness, these thoughts do not automatically *cause* us to behave in certain ways! We humans have the capacity to detach from what we think, say, hear, and read. We aren't robots programmed to follow certain rules. We have the ability to distance ourselves from language, unhook from evaluations, and disengage from the tyranny of problematic thoughts. This skill isn't often learned well in childhood, but it's hinted at in the phrase, "Sticks and stones may break my bones, but words will never hurt me." Of course, we know words can be powerful and can hurt our feelings (and even be traumatic)—but the skill of noticing is learning to distance yourself from unhelpful language, which is something that's more possible than you may think.

The age-old encouragement in mindfulness training to "notice your thoughts as if they were leaves on a stream" speaks to what the Noticing skill is on the MAP. Learning to simply observe the thoughts that pop up in your life—and to treat them with more curiosity and less urgency—can help you take actions that are more values-oriented and flexible. This is why the MAP gives specific instructions on the practice of engaging in mindful action, unhindered by distractions, which is a critical component to psychological flexibility.

| Noticing | Observe thoughts that arise while moving forward with valued actions. Let those thoughts go if they are not helpful. Treat distracting thoughts as disconnected from action while choosing to act in a meaningful manner. | |

A Query About Noticing

What thoughts arise when you start doing the things that are important to you? Early childhood conditioning and crummy things said to you by adults can stick with you. What descriptions and evaluations of the world around you impede you from doing what you find meaningful? Are there particular phrases that recur when you're about to start an important action? Write down the thoughts acting as obstacles. What healthy actions toward your values and goals can you take now in the presence of these thoughts?

_____

_____

_____

_____

_____

Moving Forward

Now you've been introduced to how the MAP works. We started this chapter suggesting that being able to genuinely say, "I am here now, accepting the way I feel, noticing my thoughts, while doing what I care about" is both the journey *and* the destination guided by the Mindful Action Plan. The MAP guides you toward a values-based, skillful, committed journey. It gives you a space to figure out what valued actions you wish to take and the specific smaller actions that will help you achieve those ends. It also helps you follow through on the functional skills inherent to psychological flexibility. We'll cover each of these skills in depth in chapters 4 through 9, and in the last chapter of this book, we'll bring all six of them back together to focus on how they work in combination. Most importantly, all along the way there will be exercises, examples, and opportunities to help you plan your journey with the MAP so you can continue walking along the path you've started.

Using a map without knowing where you are will prove difficult. As you prepare to use this MAP, it's a good idea to get a sense of where you stand now and what directions you'd like to go. This book is about planning your journey, but it's also about finding yourself. You'll learn more about that in the next chapter.

Part Two

Finding Your Why

CHAPTER 3

You Are Here

Knowing where you stand can help you take a step in the right direction. You start your valuable journey by getting your bearings, positioning yourself, and figuring out what destinations you desire, which routes would be meaningful to take, and how you'd like to act while on this journey. In other words, you figure out the goals, values, and characteristics related to the actions you want to take while you're living your path. To have the journey be valuable, you would engage in finding your why for these actions, and finding your way for taking steps on these actions. This chapter invites you to do some prerequisite work to support writing personal values statements in the What I Care About section of the MAP. Let's begin by exploring what's important to you in different areas of your life.

Come to this invitation for self-exploration with utter sincerity, true vulnerability, and an authentic dedication to exploring who you are, where you stand, and which way you want to go. This workbook leads you toward finding motivation, moving forward, and doing what you care about. And this chapter is not casual reading. For this workbook to have maximum impact, these next few pages will require your full attention and active participation. Set some time aside to engage with these writing exercises with as little distraction as possible.

Exploring the Domains of Your Life

The Mindful Action Plan is most effective when it fits what *you* care about. In chapter 1, we divided up the areas of our behavior into work, education, relationships, personal growth and health, and leisure. These are common categories (we'll call them "domains"), but if you have different ways of dividing your time, you're encouraged to use those unique categories. For the sake of simplicity, we'll start with those five areas:

1. **Work:** How do you contribute to your community? How do you earn funds to pay for what you care about?

2. **Education:** How do you go about improving your knowledge, skills, and career development?

3. **Relationships:** How do you engage with those you're close to, including your partner, children, family, friends, teammates, and others in your community?

4. **Personal Growth and Health:** How do you develop your personal life in terms of your well-being—physical, mental, and spiritual (whether or not you participate in organized religion)?

5. **Leisure:** How do you enjoy spending your free time—playing, engaging in hobbies or sports, and/or relaxing?

Take a few moments to write down what you do, how you do it, and what you care about in each of these domains. This is simply to get you focused on these areas, and we'll do deeper dives into your values in each area as we move forward. You may struggle to come up with something for a domain, and that's perfectly okay. If you have a newborn at home, your tech start-up just got venture capital, you're trying to save your marriage, or you're experiencing an intensely stressful school semester, you might think that some domains aren't important right now. That's fine! We still invite you to think about the domain and what you recall being important or what you hope will be important moving forward. Also keep in mind that this exercise isn't asking for a to-do list of goals, but simply asks what you do, how you do it, and what you find meaningful in each domain.

Work: _____

_____

_____

Education: _____

_____

_____

Relationships: _____

_____

_____

Personal Growth and Health: _____

_____

_____

Leisure: _____

_____

_____

Where Are You Going?

You've been on a journey for a while before realizing you might need a MAP. You probably already have certain destinations in mind, and you might already be working toward some objectives in your life. For instance, if you're enrolled in school, you might have the goal of earning a diploma. If you have a job you dislike, you might aim to get hired elsewhere and then resign. If you have a half-written manuscript for a play, getting it published and dramatized on stage is likely your desired destination. Note that these are all "observable" accomplishments—something that anyone can see has been completed. We can't tell what your goals are, but take time now to sketch out the destinations that you already have on your horizon.

Given the path that you're already on, what are the observable goals that you see and aspire to? Realistically, what is already on your path as a desired destination for these five areas?

What specific, observable goals are you currently working on when it comes to your work life?

_____

_____

_____

What specific, observable goals will you eventually aim for in your work life?

_____

_____

_____

What specific, observable goals are you currently working on when it comes to your education?

_____

_____

_____

What specific, observable goals will you eventually aim for in your education?

_____

_____

_____

What specific, observable goals are you currently working on when it comes to your relationships?

_____

_____

_____

What specific, observable goals will you eventually aim for in your relationships?

_____

_____

_____

What specific, observable goals are you currently working on when it comes to your personal growth and health?

_____

_____

_____

What specific, observable goals will you eventually aim for in your personal growth and health?

_____

_____

_____

What specific, observable goals are you currently working on when it comes to leisure?

_____

_____

_____

What specific, observable goals will you eventually aim for in leisure?

_____

_____

_____

EXERCISE: In What Direction Are You Traveling, and Why?

Why do you think you're going after those observable goals that you've been working on? What motivates your efforts in work and education tasks? What makes you try to develop your relationships and engage in activities that promote your health, growth, and leisure? In other words, why are you doing what you're doing? How do these goals relate to the values you've already identified?

Well…figuring that out is probably part of why you're holding this book, so let's do some exploring. Before getting specific, read through the following list of values-based terms and see how they relate to your motivation for aiming for some goals. Circle the words that resonate with you, and see how they spark additional thoughts. When you look at this list, what verbs excite you to think about doing? What qualities might you hope to bring to your actions in the various regions of your life?

VALUES-BASED TERMS

accomplish
accountability
adaptability
adopt
adventure
affirm
alleviate
altruism
ambition
appreciate
authenticity
balance
beauty
being the best
believe
belonging
brave
brighten
build
career
caring
cause
cheerful
choose
collaboration
collect
command
commitment
communicate
community
compassion
compete
complete
compliment
compose

conceive
confidence
connection
contentment
continue
contribution
cooperation
counsel
courage
courteous
create
cultivate
curiosity
defend
deliver
demonstrate
dignity
direct
discover
diversity
dream
drive
educate
efficiency
embrace
encourage
engage
enhance
enlighten
entertain
environment
equality
ethics
excellence
excitement

explore
express
fairness
faith
family
forgive
foster
freedom
friendly
friendship
fulfillment
fun
future
  generations
generosity
giving back
grace
gratitude
growth
harmony
heal
health
helpful
home
honesty
hope
humility
humor
improve
improvise
inclusion
independence
initiative
inspire
integrate

integrity
intuition
job security
joy
justice
kindness
knowledge
lead
leadership
learning
legacy
leisure
love
loyal
making a
  difference
master
mature
measure
mediate
mindful
motivate
move
nature
nurture
openness
optimism
order
organize
parenting
participate
patience
patriotism
peace
perform

perseverance
play
possess
power
practice
praise
present
pride
progress
promise
promote
provide
receive
reclaim
recognition
reduce
refine
reflect
reform
relate
relax
release
reliability
remember
renew
resonate
resourceful-
  ness
respect
responsibility
restore
reverent
risk-taking
sacrifice
safety

save
security
self-discipline
self-expression
self-respect
service
share
simplicity
solidarity
spirituality
sportsmanship
stability
success
support
surrender
sustain
teamwork
thrifty
tradition
transcend
travel
trust
trustworthy
truth
understanding
uniqueness
validate
vision
volunteer
vulnerability
wealth
well-being
wisdom
work
worship

What words stuck with you? Can you select ten words as emblematic about the way you choose to live your life? Maybe combinations or variations of these words come to mind (like "creating beauty" or "kindness in parenting"). Maybe you started looking for a particular cherished value, but you didn't see it in this group. That's fine—you can certainly add that to your list. Jot down your top words and phrases in the spaces below.

My top words and phrases:

In this exercise, you likely selected some actions and some qualities of action that capture what you consider to be important in what you do (and how you do it), such as being kind, compassionate, mindful, generous, and so on. These actions might cross many aspects of life—*create* or *educate* can be an activity that you do in your life as a parent, in your work life, and also in your leisure time, for example. You can also go deeper with respect to qualities you may have chosen and explore what behaviors relate to them that indicate what you value. For example, what does it mean to value kindness? What does that look like in your actions as a friend, a coworker, or a neighbor? Values describe *patterns* of activities, not necessarily specific activities. They reflect the manner in which you want to travel on your path.

Now that you've selected meaningful words to work with, we'll continue the process of finding your why in each life domain. Let's see which values resonate with what you're doing. Also consider why you'd put together an action plan to live your life in these directions and with these qualities of action. Truly dedicate time to exploring each of these areas of your life.

Work

You probably read a few words on the Values-Based Terms list that resonated with the notes you made earlier. You may have started thinking about how your work life measures up to what you really care about. Now let's dive deeper. We're going to go about this in two ways, because work means different things to different people.

WORKING FOR THE MONEY

For over a decade, DJ has consulted with organizations in order to improve performance by helping workers find their why. He's learned that when you ask people why they work, they often say, "For the money!" You may have a similar viewpoint—that's totally understandable. But then follow up with these questions: "Why do you *need* the money?" and "Why do you *want* the money?" This gets you closer to finding your why. The answers can start out superficially, like "to pay bills." But when you continue to ask "why," eventually you articulate a bedrock value—the answer to "why" stops at something that can't be explained but is rather just felt without a particular reason.

For instance, you might continue with this trajectory: "…so I can keep my house…so I have shelter…so I stay healthy." Or maybe: "… so that I have food in the house…so my kids eat…so they stay healthy…so they continue to grow and thrive." And you can even drill down on that last reason: "Why do you want them to grow and thrive?" Ultimately, the "why" for doing some jobs can be simply the need to provide for your own basic needs and because you love other people. And when you're having a tough day at work, resonating with love and care for others is powerfully supportive and gratifying. This is why we want to help you with finding your why for making money.

Why do you work? Ask "why" after each answer, and drill down until you find a bedrock value.

_____

_____

_____

_____

_____

_____

BEYOND THE MONEY

Many people are fortunate to have reasons for working beyond earning money, and clarifying why they work in a particular way can support them even when things become intensely difficult at work. If you look carefully at the examples above, you'll see answers with "to _____ so _____."

Early in DJ's consulting career, he asked a bartender, "Why do you work?" and the person replied very quickly, "To provide a fun and enjoyable situation so that people can unwind, socialize, and connect with others." The answer wasn't about the hourly wage, the tips, or the discount on pub food; instead, it was about seeing something meaningful come from his efforts. In another example, DJ once visited an insulated glass company. He asked a window manufacturing associate, "Why do you work?" to which she replied, "To make the highest-quality windows for people's homes so that the light comes in and the cold stays out!" In some jobs, seeing meaningful outcomes is the primary remuneration for our work. If you look at the work of volunteers and folks who serve in nonprofit organizations, much of the time the "why" has to be beyond the money. People choose to do something effortful so that meaningful outcomes and processes occur. This truly is values-based work because the "pay" is simply their gratification in the work.

Using these examples, the Values-Based Terms list above, and your reflections, go beyond the money, and answer this question: "Why do I work?" Take a look at the tasks you perform and the contributions you make. Sure, you may get paid for it, but that's because someone else finds value in what you're doing. What is it about what you're doing that has such value? See if you can sharpen the answer of why you work to articulate a very clear statement, as in the previous examples. Include descriptions of the actions that are important to you as well as the qualities or characteristics of those actions that you value.

_____

_____

_____

_____

_____

_____

Education

"You learn something new every day!" If you're lucky, that old phrase is true, and if you're purposeful with your education, you can ensure that it will be true. Even if you haven't been in a classroom in many years, you can still be aware of the lessons life has to offer and the knowledge inherent in all subjects you care about. Clearly, just by reading this book, you have some motivation for becoming educated in intentional living and mindful action. Why? Why do you want to learn about certain topics, and why are they meaningful to you?

THE TURNING POINT LESSON

Think back on your life, and recall some of the "aha" moments you've experienced. Can you remember a time when you had an epiphany? Was there a time when something really struck you, and you wanted to know more about it, and, in fact, the topic consumed you for a while? These types of events, unique to your journey, might have occurred in childhood when you were at school or participating in a youth organization or a sports team. Maybe your "aha" came later in life as you were finding your vocation and career path. Can you remember a "lightbulb moment" when something lit up your interest? Record some of those memories below.

_____

_____

_____

_____

_____

Let's look a bit further. What fascinates you? Can you think of a time when you were enthralled by a topic? What was it, and how did it feel to explore that topic and learn more?

_____

_____

_____

_____

Sometimes our learning is less than fascinating and enthralling, but we value it highly because it's linked to other important areas of our lives. For instance, perhaps you pursue education in some area related to your job, and while it isn't mesmerizing, you study it nonetheless because it's related to other meaningful things in your life. Given all of these considerations, and after reviewing the list of values-based terms and what you wrote previously for this area, write a statement below saying, "I pursue further education to learn about _____, in order to _____."

_____

_____

_____

Relationships

To love one another is one of humankind's greatest callings. Arguably the most important domain of our existence is our relationship with other people. How we relate to partners, family, friends, colleagues, neighbors, and strangers is influenced by our values.

From our perspective, you're on a journey with every single person on this planet—but let's get more specific. Who are your fellow travelers and how would you choose to interact with them? Think about the people you regularly interact with, and how you want to be in relationship with them.

EXERCISE: Your 80th Birthday Party

When you turn eighty years old, there will be cause for celebration. Imagine the party you could have, and who you would like to host this monumental event. Extend your imagination beyond who would likely be there from a practical point of view, and fantasize about who you'd enjoy having there. Now at this delightful festivity, people will likely reminisce about your past actions, and give toasts and speeches in your honor. Take time with this exercise to look at two areas of valuing: what you care about in your life, and how you treat other people during it.

These folks know you, so what do you want them to say about their interactions with you in the past? What memories of you do they cherish? Different people will tell stories about your adventures (or misadventures), the principles you stood for, and the impact you had on them and the world. What do you want them to say?

Think about someone you're incredibly close to, and what you hope they believe is important to you. What would you like them to say at the party? Think about someone else you're closely related to and consider what you'd like them to say about you. What would you like your children to say? (Even if you don't have any children now, use your imagination.) What would you like your colleagues, friends, and neighbors to say about how you act and what you care about? At this celebration, what values are being celebrated? What do you stand for so obviously that other people can witness it? Consider each of these different types of relationships and thoughtfully consider how you would like these people to think about you and your values.

Relationship	What do you want them to say about your personal values and what is important in your life?	What do you hope they will say about how you treated them in your relationship?
Intimate partner		
Children		
Family member		
Friend		
Friend		
Colleague/Coworker		
Neighbor		

Look for a theme in these answers. Is there a set of values that you'd like to demonstrate in each one of these relationships? If this kind of purposeful action on your part keeps popping up in different areas of your life, you're starting to clarify your values—you're finding your why.

This exercise might have been very difficult. Perhaps you have a history of child abuse, recently broke up with a significant other, are estranged from your kids, or find yourself lonely and having a hard time making friends. Overall, this exercise is about uncovering your values—patterns of your chosen actions—when interacting with other people. Perhaps your current relationships have been tarnished and are complicated. This exercise asks how you would choose to be in relationships. Even in the presence of any resentment, bitterness, or sadness you might feel, if you could accept those feelings, how would you choose to behave in interpersonal relationships if you were more psychologically flexible?

Personal Growth and Health

After considering your relationships with other people, think about the most important relationship you have—the one with yourself! When it comes to taking care of *you*, what's important? This is an incredibly broad topic because personal goals can range from making minor adjustments, such as taking extra time to engage in daily exercise, to incredibly major changes, like getting out of an abusive relationship, moving away, or starting a career so that you can maintain your newfound independence. Personal growth and health could include meditating to aid in overcoming depression. The goals themselves are for you to choose, and in this section, we invite you to work on *why* those are important personal goals.

EXERCISE: Visualizing Valued Directions

Imagine you could fashion how you lived your life so that you could truly cherish it. We're not inviting you to fantasize about fancy cars and luxury homes, but rather to envision a life well lived with the resources available. If you could live your life in a meaningful, purposeful way, how would you choose to act? What parts of your habits and daily activities would you keep and expand upon, and which ones would you pitch? Take a few moments to visualize what your life would look like if you were living this way. Is there an area of growth that you would like to nurture in your life?

I aim to grow in the area of _____ because I really care

about _____.

Write your personal-growth values statement:

_____

_____

_____

_____

Leisure

Mindful action can also occur when you're purely enjoying your life. Whether you're on a thrill-seeking adventure or relaxing in a hammock, being present and aware makes it much more enjoyable. Well-spent leisure time helps lower stress, reduces depression and anxiety, and contributes to an overall quality of life, and the way to optimize this is to choose leisure activities that recharge *your* batteries. When you have time away from traditional responsibilities, you can engage in enjoyable, fun activities, and these are influenced by values. Some people play cards with their neighbors, while others take a solo hike in the mountains, and sometimes both activities are in the bandwidth of leisure for the same person, just at different times. What floats your boat, so to speak?

EXERCISE: Meaningful Pleasure

Think of a time when you genuinely focused on a sense of meaningful pleasure. This could be an episode of "me time" when you engaged in a relaxing and satisfying hobby, or when you were intensely active in the middle of a team sport. Remember a time when you were truly in the moment because you gained pleasure while doing that particular action. Recall a time when you said, "Wow, I really love doing this!" Tailor the following sentence to fit you:

I really like spending my leisure time doing _____ because I really care

about _____.

How do you enjoy spending your time, and why?

_____

_____

_____

_____

You just looked at work, education, relationships, personal growth and health, and leisure as different domains of your life. Each domain reflects your values in a particular way. The exercises you've done can also be applied to other areas to provide new insights. For example, you could utilize the 80th Birthday Party exercise to your clarify work values or the Turning Point Lesson exercise to illuminate your leisure values. Use these exercises flexibly for best results: your Mindful Action Plan can be focused on any or all of these areas in your life.

Finding Your Way: The Life Atlas

An atlas is a collection of maps, and in this workbook, the Life Atlas is your collection of MAPs. (The Life Atlas is available for download at http://www.newharbinger.com/50713.) Since you've just finished clarifying what's important in valued domains of your life, we anticipate you'll eventually map out several different plans of action—reflecting different goals and values in different domains. Prior to developing those plans, let's establish which domains are important to you and look at how you're doing in each one.

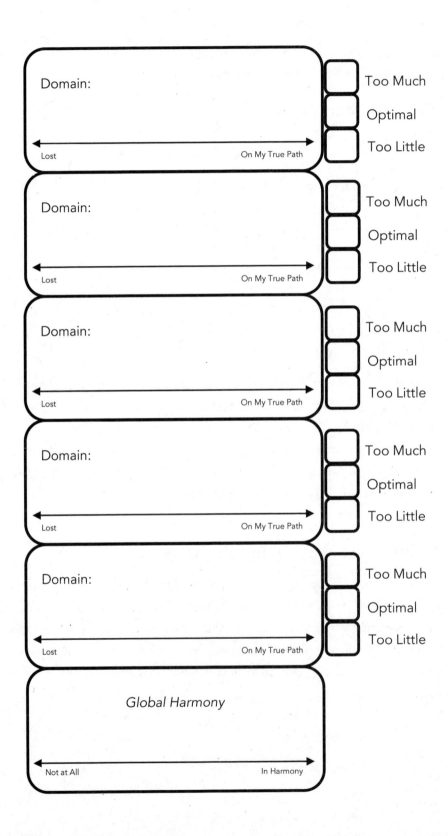

EXERCISE: Life Atlas Locations

Take a look at your Life Atlas, which gives you a global picture of your important domains. Write those domains you chose earlier (for example, work, education, relationships, personal growth and health, and leisure) in each "Domain" box. You can always come back to this atlas and adjust it as we explore the terrain later. And, if you want to draw your own map, or put your domains in different places, by all means, go for it! All that matters right now is that you're beginning to get a picture of what's important to you on your life's journey.

Now consider how well your actions in these domains reflect the values you identified as being important. Place an X on the line indicating how you're doing right now. On the "Lost" end, you feel disoriented, confused, and stuck. The things you're doing on a daily basis don't reflect what's important to you, and you don't even know how to get to the path you want to be on. At the other end, you consider yourself "On My True Path," so your actions solidly align with your values, and every step is meaningful and purposeful.

How close are you to staying on track with your meaningful, psychologically flexible journey? You'll be able to rate just how well you're engaging in mindful action by taking a look at how your Life Atlas ratings change from time to time. When the ratings for the different areas of your life slide over to the "On My True Path" side of the spectrum, you're demonstrating genuine psychological flexibility. There may be days when you feel closer or further from your path—for now, just place an X to show where you are today.

Next, take an aerial view of your Life Atlas. You are a whole person after all, and not neatly divided up into separate and isolated experiences. Are there domains that seem to be taking over your life? As you seek to have a meaningful journey, rate the amount of time you spend in each domain as "Too Much," "Optimal," or "Too Little."

At the bottom of the Life Atlas is a scale labeled "Global Harmony." Rate the level of harmony you feel in your whole life right now. On one end, the domains of your life are "Not at All" in harmony—one may take up all your time in ways that aren't your priorities, or you may find it difficult to "switch gears" from work to leisure or vice versa. On the other end, harmony reigns—you are "In Harmony," ideally engaged in each domain and smoothly traveling among them.

The Life Atlas provides a viewpoint for a life well lived, as defined by you. It also gives you perspective on what's most meaningful to you and how optimally immersed you are in what you care about.

Moving Forward

Now that you've completed the exercises in this chapter, take a deep breath, relax, and slowly exhale. If you're like us, the Life Atlas exercise might have been a bit tough to do. It might have distressed you if you realized you've been walking the wrong direction for a while, or that you've just been sitting on a rock by the side of the road for a long time. But keep in mind what you have done: you articulated what you care about and how much you're acting in the service of those values. So now that you've established where you are, you can explore how to get to where you want to go. The MAP can help you take the next steps on your life's adventure and to build psychological flexibility skills to keep you on your path even when you run into obstacles along the way.

This chapter asked a lot of questions, and we have one more to ask. But first, recall this statement: "I am here now, accepting the way I feel, noticing my thoughts, while doing what I care about." Can you say that statement to yourself? If you can, that's fantastic, and the rest of the book will help you maintain this level of psychological flexibility. If you can't, that's just fine—the rest of the book will help you build the skills that will support your efforts in mindful action.

CHAPTER 4

What I Care About

In the last chapter, you used the Life Atlas to orient yourself on your path and started working on finding your *why*—your valued actions and qualities giving your life meaning. You also started the journey of finding your *way*—where you are with respect to living in alignment with those values, how skillfully you act while moving through the domains of your life, and how well harmonized those domains are. Now, over the course of the next six chapters, we'll dive more deeply into each of the six key skill areas of the MAP, beginning with the central focus of doing what you care about. In this chapter, you'll further clarify your values and learn a bit more about how values statements work to guide you on your journey.

A Piece of the MAP: What I Care About

What I Care About	Values-Based Motivation	
	Personal Values: Describe your motivation for engaging in your chosen actions and why you aim for optimal performance.	

As mentioned in chapter 2, we start using the MAP by looking at the What I Care About section. Given all the work that you just did in the last chapter, can you envision how you would use this part of the checklist? Note that this section of the MAP is right under the To-Do List, demonstrating that

What I Care About provides a supporting foundation for doing chosen actions. You'll be using this section of the Mindful Action Plan to articulate what's meaningful about all the things on your to-do list. Lots of people use to-do lists, but how often do they include "why I'm doing this" on the list? This section provides the motivation to stay dedicated to executing all the tasks from your list. These are the values that support your committed actions. In fact, acceptance and commitment therapy highlights the component of Values in the same manner that the MAP discusses What I Care About.

Considerations for Values Explorations

As you work on this chapter, we'd like you to keep a few things in mind about values. First, when you construct a statement of your values and note it in the What I Care About section of the MAP, your statement is obviously made up of words, but those words are empty without the doing. Values describe an ongoing, ever-changing pattern of activity. We've described them before as a "direction" you might go (like a North Star to guide you), but this doesn't mean that values are *just* a direction; they're also meant to be qualities you translate into actions—qualities that actively shape the actions you do and don't take. Ultimately, we're talking not just about static values you might claim to hold, but about valu*ing* as a behavior: acting in line with the values you hold.

Next, values are something that you get to *choose* for yourself—no one but you can know what's truly important to you. We can't tell you, your friends and family can't tell you (though they might try), and while our culture gives all of us plenty of messages about what we "should" find important, we don't necessarily have to agree with those. In your life journey, you get to decide where to go and how to get there. That might be very much in line with the values of your family or community, or it might not. Of course, we're certainly not saying that to live in line with your values you *have* to be a rebel. In fact, if you're "rebelling" just for the sake of *not* doing what is expected, that probably isn't really choosing a valued direction either. If you're truly choosing, then rebellion or conformity occurs for a thoughtfully considered purpose and makes your life meaningful.

Finally, there's no one "right" way to construct your statements about what's important to you, any more than there is some "right" set of values. We'll give you suggestions and tools to help you, but ultimately the only thing that matters is that your statements of what you care about resonate deeply with the way you want to live your life. What was it like for you to articulate what was important in each of those domains of life in your Life Atlas? Was it a struggle, or were you simply listing the way you were actually living? Take another perspective now: If you were the main character in the travelogue of your life, would readers be able to describe what's important to you? Would they observe you doing the actions you care about? You may have a quick answer to these questions, or you may struggle to find the right words—in either case, there is likely more of the story to write. Let's begin to write it.

Throughout this book, we'll be following several individuals on their journeys with the MAP. The first, Ella, has been in a situation you might find familiar—unsure if the life she's living is one informed by her deepest values.

● *Ella's Story*

Ella, previously an outstanding student, found herself struggling to find motivation to continue her studies. She was just a few years into her nursing program, on her way to becoming a pediatric nurse. When she first enrolled, Ella thought this was her dream. She'd spent summers in high school working as an administrative assistant in a pediatric practice owned by her father's cousin, and she continues to work there part-time while in school. She had been promised a nursing job there once she completed her licensing requirements. Her parents instilled in her the importance of hard work and having a job with stability and security, and she did enjoy helping others. But now in her third year of school, she's struggling to get to classes on time, let alone getting assignments completed, and she's been putting off signing up for the next semester's course requirements. She wonders if maybe she's not cut out for college at all. When she stands back and looks at herself and her life, she feels lost—very far from her path—and not really "herself."

On the advice of a trusted professor, Ella met with a counselor at her university's wellness center. The counselor asked her what was important to her and had her start the Life Atlas exercise (as you did in the last chapter). Ella identified school/career, family, friendships, recreation/travel, and health as domains that really mattered to her. She thought about what she wanted in her career and in her life as a whole as well as the qualities that are important in her vocation, relationships, and life outside of school. What did she dream of doing after she finished her degree? What did she care about? And how close was she to the path she wanted to take in life? No one had ever genuinely asked Ella these kinds of questions before, and she struggled to come up with something that felt true. Ella confessed that sometimes she wanted to just chuck it all and go see the world.

As Ella thought about how she wanted to be and what she wanted to do, she looked at a list of values-related words (as you also did). These words resonated with her: "command," "direct," "lead," "heal," "helpful," as well as "joy" and "travel." She also added "challenging" and "spontaneous" to her list. When she considered all these words together, she felt both inspired by how abundant life could be, and she also felt sad—she felt so far away from these qualities.

Although a job as a pediatric nurse in her cousin's office would involve lots of healing and helping, some of the values she'd picked weren't there. In fact, working in a pediatric practice didn't spark much excitement or a sense of purpose at all. There would definitely be no directing or commanding while working at the family business, and nothing about the job felt challenging, joyful, or spontaneous. She looked at the words she'd written down and wondered how she could ever bring all these qualities into her life. At the same time, she felt that it might be possible to do so—maybe she could figure out how to find her path now that she knew a bit more of what she was looking for.

Look at your Life Atlas. Which domain did you rate as furthest from "On My True Path"? Which actions related to that domain feel poorly aligned with your values? In the last chapter, what did you write when asked what you found meaningful in that lagging domain? With more reflection, can you add to that statement or make any changes to it? Go ahead and do that now, and write your response below. The clearer your why, the easier it will be to find your way back to your path. (Of course, if you'd like to do this for more than one domain, go right ahead!)

Domain: _____

Values statement: _____

_____

_____

Valuing Is Caring

In the last chapter, you repeatedly questioned "why" you do things, reminiscing about a turning point in your life, imagining how you want your 80th birthday party to go, and visualizing a life well lived. You can also discover what you value by appreciating what worries you, where you hurt, and what you're afraid of. Emotional pain occurs when you lose something meaningful and important in your life, even when you anticipate such a loss or see it occurring for others. For instance, if you're a parent, you probably find it gut-wrenching to watch news stories or movies where something bad happens to children. If you've been preparing for an important job interview, you might feel anxious and worried. However, if you didn't care about the job or your children, you probably wouldn't be worried! You hurt when you care, which is the flipside of values. The fact that you care dignifies the difficulty of learning to accept your emotions.

Caring, Emotions, and Values

When you think about the different domains of your life, particularly that one you identified where you feel far from your path, is there anything that you worry about or find painful? Write out your concerns and indicate what's painful and anxiety provoking for you:

_____

_____

_____

_____

_____

What does that tell you about what's important to you? How do your worries link to your chosen values?

_____

_____

_____

_____

_____

Knowing that you feel heightened emotions around certain topics is a clue that you're contacting things that are vital to your life. Let's try this: If you could not visit this domain on your Life Atlas, what would you miss? What would be painful for you to miss out on? Note your observations, within the context of the values statements you developed in the last chapter.

What I don't want to miss out on: _____

_____

_____

_____

_____

Valuing Is Choosing

We've been saying you get to choose your values throughout this book, and as behavioral scientists we mean something special when we talk about choosing. Freely choosing means what you're doing is not motivated primarily by the need to escape from difficult, painful, or uncomfortable events. Valuing isn't just about avoiding things that feel bad, or accessing something enticing in the short-term that also has big long-term drawbacks. When we talk about freely choosing something, we mean our motivation is based on considering the outcomes of that choice, and that the long-term outcomes of the choice are beneficial in some way. Valuing involves deliberately choosing to engage in the activities right here and now that are most meaningful in the long term, whether or not they have short-term difficulties. A good first step to choosing your actions more deliberately is to observe how and where you spend your time now.

For example, when Ella thought about a typical day and week in her life, she saw that she spent a great deal of time watching action movies, browsing travel sites online, and going out with her friends. She also spent a lot of time *not* doing what she needed to do for school. She also saw that she avoided talking to her family. When she looked at her Life Atlas exercise, she could see she prioritized socializing and engaging in leisure activities (and wondered, *Does binge-watching TV shows count as "leisure?"*). Ella saw that she engaged in some values-based behaviors, but the Global Harmony was off. She also saw that she was doing a lot of those activities so she wouldn't have to think about school and the future of her career. And none of those activities really lined up well with the values-based terms she'd selected as important and meaningful.

EXERCISE: Am I Living in Line with My Values?

Think about today and the past week. Look back to your Life Atlas. Are you spending "Too Much" of your time in a domain where you're feeling lost? Are you spending "Optimal" time where you're on your true path or "Too Little" time doing what you care about? Do you have activities you want to do, but aren't? Do you have things you don't want to do, but you do them quite a bit? Reflect and review the Global Harmony portion of your Life Atlas.

Now, look at the template below—with one side for "I spend too much time…" and the other for "I don't spend enough time…" Write everything you notice below—the words that initially come to mind and any other thoughts that arise as you do this exercise. Perhaps you'll notice something difficult (a thought or an emotion) showing up around things you aren't choosing.

I spend too much time...	I don't spend enough time...

Think about your reasons for engaging or not engaging in each of these activities: What did you get from the activities you did "Too Much" of? What would you hope to get from those you spent "Too Little" time on?

What would it mean to embody the qualities and actions you identified previously within these areas of your life? When you think about the different domains, how do the words and phrases that you picked show up in how you travel through each part of your life? Can you think of ways those values could be a part of the activities you do in a way that gets you closer to your path? Feel free to add more to your values statements from the previous chapter; you don't have to be restricted to just a few statements of what you care about. Make some notes below about your experience of this exercise.

Choosing Your Own Path

Figuring out what's personally valuable is a critical task that begins in childhood, carries through adolescence as young people explore the world separate from their families, and continues throughout our lives. It's often very difficult for young people like Ella to articulate what's uniquely important to them. If you ask teens questions like "What is important to you?," you'll often get answers like "doing well in school" or "being kind to others." These are likely statements of what's *supposed* to be important. If you have almost automatic responses to a question about "What do you value?" or "What is important to you in life?" this might be a clue that there's more to figure out. It might be important to separate a "supposed to" statement from what is truly valued.

Of course, we're not saying that automatic responses are always untrue or bad. Those qualities that come to mind immediately or automatically—for instance, if you're a parent, "being a good parent"—are almost certainly very important to you; we aren't saying that something like "being a good parent" can't be a value even if it's something that society tells us is important. Most of us value common activities, like contributing in some way to our communities, spending time with our social group, or maintaining our health. But we encourage you to dig deeper than those broad statements to get at the heart of the value for *you*.

If No One Was Watching

Review the values statements that you've been authoring in this workbook. Now ask yourself, *Would I call this my value if I couldn't tell anyone else that this was important to me?* Take a few moments to consider this question and write your thoughts below.

_____

_____

_____

_____

_____

Next, ask yourself, *Would I continue to do this if no one knew I was doing it?* What if you couldn't post about it on social media, tell your parents about the accomplishment, or explain what you've been doing to your friends?

_____

_____

_____

_____

_____

Take some time now to reconsider and revise any statements that are impactful for you.

When you look at your values statements and the activities that you do, ask yourself, *Am I following the directions someone else put on my Life Atlas, or am I choosing these directions freely?*

Look at the values you've been writing in the different domains of your life. As you've been writing, have you been telling yourself you "have to" or "really should" do more or less of these activities? If you didn't choose to do these valued activities, do you believe someone else would be mad or disappointed? Are you choosing these actions because someone else will reward you with praise, or are you *freely choosing* these valued activities? Write your thoughts below.

_____

_____

_____

_____

_____

_____

Ultimately, when you construct statements to capture what's important and meaningful to you, consider carefully whether or not these are specifically meaningful to *you* or if they represent something you think "should" be important. When you engage in activities that are truly meaningful to you, the actions may be difficult, even painful, but it's unlikely that they'll feel like a boring chore to be checked off the to-do list.

Let's look at a commonly stated value: being healthy and fit. Lots of us probably have noted some value related to our health, like "Being fit so I can enjoy being active with my kid and future grandkids." Siri had this value written on her MAP, linked to a "to-do" of going to the pool to swim. Several times a week, she dragged herself off to the gym, often feeling guilty that she wasn't doing something else but reminding herself that "being healthy and fit is important." Once she was swimming, she thoroughly enjoyed the time in the pool, but getting there was always a big chore. She didn't even seem to be losing any weight (one of the goals she had around the value of being healthy and fit), and she went less and less. She finally realized that the value of swimming for her wasn't at all about being fit. She realized that while swimming would be helpful for fitness, the real value was genuinely in the doing of the activity: the time to think, to not be in contact with the busy outside world, to be alone, and to stretch both her body and mind. When she saw swimming as a gift of meditative reflective time to herself, going to the pool became precious, something she "got to do," not something she "had to do." She connected the activity to a value she could embody in every moment rather than something she was supposed to want to be. She found the value that was unique to *her* life, not someone else's.

Now that you've learned more about valuing, you might begin revising the valued domains on your Life Atlas. Maybe the five domains we suggested aren't really yours! Consider rephrasing them if they don't fit *you*. For example, Siri's partner (an artist) labeled his domains with completely different categories than the ones we listed. He realized identifying his core values of "creativity" and "collaboration" was better captured by the phrase "making art" rather than "work." Notice that earlier, Ella identified phrases that worked better for her too, like combining "school/career" as a domain rather than having separate "work" and "education" domains, and separating out a domain for "family" from a domain for "friendships" rather than having one "relationships" domain. Just because we suggested five categories doesn't mean they're right for you.

● Ella's Story

When Ella reflected on what she was doing with her time, and why she was in the program she was in, she realized her decisions had been driven by what was important to her fairly traditional parents: having a secure and stable job (and one they believed was appropriate for a woman), and a career involving nurturing and caring for others (such as being a nurse or a kindergarten teacher like her mom). Yet, when Ella thought about not *doing something in medicine, that pained her too. She didn't want to reject this career simply because her parents wanted it for her. She realized working in medicine was truly important to her. She did value helping others and considered herself good in a crisis. She just didn't want to be working all her life as a nurse in a pediatrician's office.*

Ella decided she needed to explore alternate paths and to discover how it feels to work in a challenging position that involves taking charge of things. She wondered, Maybe an emergency room nurse? Ella's counselor also suggested she review her coursework with fresh eyes, finding the challenge in it and how it might be used in other settings. Ella started thinking more about including travel in her career. A friend told her about travel nursing jobs, but she had rejected it, knowing that her parents wouldn't approve. Was it wasting time to take a look at that option again? Ella felt excited, took stock of just how far behind she was in her coursework, and made an action plan to catch up.

Values Versus Goals

When we think of important actions to do, specific achievements come to mind: winning a championship, getting a particular job, having kids, or swimming a mile. You wrote some of these goals down for yourself earlier, and, when you thought about why you might want to do more or less of certain activities, you might have thought about these kinds of goals. Goals are certainly important, but as you've already seen, valuing is about more than goals. Valuing is about the journey itself, not just the destinations you might reach along the way. Values reflect the broad qualities that steer you toward discrete goals.

For instance, the goal "winning a championship" may be motivated by personal qualities and actions like "being the best," "compete," and "wholeheartedness"—and these values give purpose to the pursuit of that goal. When you're really valuing—that is, doing what you care about—it's not a crushing defeat if you fail to achieve your goal. An athlete who doesn't win a championship doesn't quit the sport. Why? Because it's about the doing, not just the achieving.

To dig into values, we can think about what's beyond the goal, just as you thought "beyond the money" when first examining your values with respect to work. Why do you want to achieve that goal? What's important in the process of the work you do to achieve that goal? What are you hoping to explore on your journey, and what qualities do you hope characterize your travel? Valuing lets you be present on the path: every step lets you inhabit your valued way of action.

If you have a hard time thinking past your goal as the most important issue, then imagine that a magician simply arranged for you to achieve the outcome. This is like being teleported to your destination instead of traveling on the journey. While you might be relieved to have arrived, you've missed out on something you could've experienced along the way. If you planned to hike a trail down the Grand Canyon, but you were magically transported to the base without experiencing nature's beauty, you'd very likely be disappointed to be at the bottom so quickly and easily. Valuing is about the journey, not the destination.

Distinguishing Values from Goals

Look at the values statements you came up with earlier. Are any of them things you could accomplish and be done with? Mark these as possible *goals*, and we'll come back to them in the next chapter.

Also take a look at the goals you already identified. Then think about this: What would be your big reason for accomplishing those goals? What would you want to do or learn in the process? What do you want to explore while you're there? See if you can construct a statement that describes the value inherent in that journey—the direction or the quality of the path rather than the destination. Write your statement below.

As Ella completed this exercise for her "school/career" domain, she noticed she wrote down some possible goals like "graduate and become a registered nurse" and "travel the Southwest." To come up with a better values statement, she went back to consider what was at the heart of each of these goals—what the goals would represent for her if she were able to achieve them. With respect to her career, she identified this: "I value being a leader, helping and healing others, and challenging myself." In other domains, she clarified these values: "I value honesty in loving relationships and helping my family" and "I value spontaneity and connecting with joy and creative exploration through meeting new people and visiting new places."

Now revisit the values statements for each of the domains you've chosen to focus on. Take care to make sure they're true values statements, not goals, and continue to refine them so they clearly point you in the direction you want to go.

Domain: _____

Values statement: _____

Domain: _____

Values statement: _____

Domain: _____

Values statement: _____

_____

Domain: _____

Values statement: _____

_____

Domain: _____

Values statement: _____

_____

Valuing Helps When the Path Is Hard

If you had a magic compass that automatically pointed you in the direction of what was most important, and if the path were flat and clear and you could always see the horizon, you wouldn't need a map. However, we assume you're with us on the journey of this book because you've gotten a bit lost and stuck, or you aren't moving forward on your path as quickly or as well as you would like to, or because you sense you could use some guidance for the journey of life. This is totally normal; doing things that are deeply important, as you're doing now, is typically difficult.

We can also feel lost or stuck in periods of change, such as starting a new job or school or business, becoming a parent, losing a loved one, or experiencing significant illness. Sometimes big changes leave you feeling like a tornado picked you up off your path and set you down somewhere in the middle of the forest. Having clarity around your values, such as knowing what matters to you and why you were on that path in the first place, helps you find your way back—or perhaps even forge a new path.

There's no one right way to construct a values statement. What matters is how the statement resonates with the way you most wish to live your life. This is the power of language: it can transform how we feel about events, including unpleasant ones. Values statements can motivate you to walk a hard path and transform difficulty and pain into meaning and purpose. They can assist you both during agonizing experiences like changing careers or going through a divorce, and minor annoyances like dealing with computer mishaps or getting stuck in traffic.

For example, as a self-employed practitioner, Siri often put off doing various administrative tasks, like billing and paperwork. She tried to tie this work to some of her values around clients, like helping children and families, but it still felt like a chore. She avoided it at all costs and then ended up slogging through the work far too late. When she realized that the values statements she had connected to administrative tasks were *not* changing how she felt, she did some deeper thinking and discovered that the real value and purpose for these tasks was connected to other values she held: independence and autonomy. If she wanted to enjoy the freedom and flexibility of being her own boss, she had to do the admin. She still isn't overjoyed about doing paperwork, but it does feel different. Whenever she sits down to tackle those administrative tasks, she's reminded of how grateful she is to be able to have flexibility and independence in her work, and how they feel like less of a chore. This makes her more willing to engage in doing the work. (We'll talk more about the importance of willingness in chapter 7.)

Of course, there are many mundane tasks that are simply associated with living life, and you don't need to tie absolutely everything you do to some critically important value! It's not a contest to see how many minutes a day you can spend in "meaningful" activity or how "purposeful" taking out the trash can be. Nonetheless, where you can see meaning and purpose, even in everyday chores, you may find your feelings about those activities shifting. Valuing has an emotional impact that cannot be underestimated, which is why we began teaching you how to use the MAP with this section. When you describe your motivation for engaging in your chosen actions and why you aim for optimal performance, you're more likely to change how you feel about doing hard things.

⬡ Ella's Story

Once Ella had clarified her values, she felt better about working to catch up on her classes. Even though it seemed overwhelming, she created a MAP to help her get back on track. She met with the counselor a few more times and realized the hardest part of her new plan would be talking to her parents about her choices. When she had explored her values in the domain of "family," she had identified "honesty in loving relationships" as being very important to her, but she could see that, although she hadn't been lying to her parents, she also hadn't been forthright about what was going on for her. She was afraid that they wouldn't understand and would think she was ungrateful and silly. She also knew that on a fundamental level, they shared her value of being honest in relationships—they'd always been honest with her about what they thought and expected of her, even when those things weren't necessarily what she herself might've wanted to hear.

She wrote out a reminder for herself: "I will talk to my family about changing my career path, because I value honesty in my relationship with them, and they value honesty in their relationship with me." She also tailored the Mindful Action Plan statement just for herself: "I am here now, accepting my feelings of fear and guilt, noticing my thoughts about what my parents might say, while doing what I care about." She felt terrified to have the conversation, but also deeply felt how important it was to do, and she texted her mom about meeting for dinner that weekend.

Realigning Activities and Values

Return to your Life Atlas. Consider again one of the domains where you feel furthest from the mark in terms of living your values.

Identify an activity from one of your previous lists that matches with a specific value in this domain, but that you haven't been readily engaging in. This might be something on your list of things you wish you did more of, or simply an activity that's been on your to-do list for a long time and you've put off doing. This is similar to the "Beyond the Money" exercise you did earlier. First, think about how you might fill in the blanks in the following sentences:

It is important to me to _____(activity/action)_____ because/so that _____(value)_____.

I value _____(value)_____, so I will _____(activity/action)_____.

For example, here's what Siri wrote:

It is important to me to <u>swim regularly</u> so that <u>I can have solitude, creativity, and time to think and move freely</u>.

I value <u>independence, autonomy, and flexibility</u>, so I will <u>complete my administrative tasks</u>.

Now, fill in your responses:

It is important to me to _____

because/so that _____

_____.

I value _____,

so I will _____.

There's no one right way to author these statements of your values and valued activities. But notice how it *feels* when you say your sentence—do your thoughts and feelings shift? The next time you have the opportunity to do this activity, return to what you've written here and observe how it feels at that time, engaging in this action with intention.

Moving Forward

In this chapter, we focused on identifying the direction for your action: what you care about. You've learned to distinguish between a value and a goal, and started to clear your path by constructing some statements about what's most important in how you live your life. You've seen how valuing can help when there are obstacles in your path, and you've identified what you want to pay more attention to. We hope that expanding your Life Atlas and filling in even just this one part of the MAP—What I Care About—has been a powerful experience. Hopefully, doing this will help you take those first steps that will lead you closer to finding and walking your most meaningful path. As you do this, remember that even if you never reach a particular destination, you're walking in the right direction and engaging in valuing with every step, because values are directions that will shape your whole life and make it meaningful and fulfilling. You're already building your psychological flexibility skills, and you've only just begun!

Part Three

Finding Your Way

CHAPTER 5

Doing

Imagine you're about to embark on a fantastic road trip. See the car as it looks from the outside. Did you imagine a family station wagon with wood paneling on the side, or a decked-out pickup truck? Or perhaps you thought of a minivan with kids buckled up in the back. Picture that vehicle with all its complexity. See the seats, stereo, and steering wheel on the inside, and a whole bunch of interconnected mechanisms under the hood. What is the most important part of this vehicle for the road trip to occur?

If you answered, "the people," you get an A+ for humanity and lovingness. If you answered, "the seatbelts," congratulations for being a compassionate and safe person. If you said "the fuel," you understand machinery—and since you just finished a chapter on clarifying your values, you might be still thinking about motivation and the stuff that makes things go.

That said, in this chapter, we argue that the most important part of this or any vehicle is "where the rubber hits the road!" This common phrase actually refers to four small parts, one on each tire that's just a few inches in area. Mechanics call this the "contact patch": the points at which tires get traction on the asphalt. The entire automobile is very complex and works together in amazing ways, especially if it is fine-tuned. But when you put all the complexity together, the car is only truly worthy if it does what a car is meant to do: get you where you want to go!

Like the car, the MAP is also complex, and the components can work together in amazing ways for you, especially if the skills are fine-tuned. But when you put all these skills together, they're only truly worthy if they help you do what the MAP is meant for: Doing! Doing your life with more purpose. Doing more of the things that you care about and less of the things that don't serve your values. Doing is where the rubber hits the road on the MAP.

A Piece of the MAP: Doing

Doing	To-Do List			

The MAP is a checklist for improving psychological flexibility, and the Doing section is a checklist for what you choose to do flexibly. In acceptance and commitment therapy, this is called "committed action." Throughout this chapter, you'll develop committed action goals, which you'll do to create a life well lived. You'll do this by acting on your clarified values. You'll list those actions or chosen behaviors in the To-Do List in the Doing section of the MAP. When you see that there's only space for ten actions on the To-Do List, you might protest, "But I have a lot to do! Why am I limited to just ten things?" You aren't limiting yourself to doing just ten things for the rest of your life, but paring your list down to just ten things will help you focus on what you have to do. This To-Do List can be used in many different ways, but you'll get more traction if you attend to a smaller set of behaviors for your action plan.

What Do You Care About Doing?

Ultimately, the work you put into articulating What I Care About, the section of the MAP that supports the Doing section, needs to be transformed into concrete actions. You can plan the greatest road trip with a map, but if the rubber doesn't hit the road, the car won't go anywhere! Likewise, you can plan a great journey with the MAP, but if you aren't doing committed actions, you're not creating a life well lived. You've already reflected on this as you've thought about activities that you spend too much and too little time on. As a result, you feel you're not fully on your true path and the Global Harmony of your life is not optimal. If you worked diligently in the last chapter, you recognize what moves you and what has meaning for you. And now, it's your time to literally move—that is, to take measurable actions, doing what moves you in valued directions along your path. We'll explore how you'll develop the To-Do List in your MAPs by refining your goals so they're smart and wise. You'll also learn to prioritize your valued actions and evaluate your progress toward a life well lived. In short, we'll focus on planning for mindful *action*.

The Mindful Action Plan assists you in being more productive, values-based, and present-focused while doing your chosen actions. The MAP also helps you embrace what you choose to do in the service of your values with greater vitality, commitment, and understanding. At the same time, this book is *not* a book on how to do something in particular, but about doing anything you want with greater flexibility and vitality.

In the exercises in the last two chapters, you identified the directions you'd like to go, so now it's time to develop the measurable outcomes for those directions—that is, the criteria that you can use to tell whether you're making progress and achieving your goals. To get a sense of what we mean by this, let's meet Ken.

● Ken's Story

Ken spent his thirties enjoying beer, bourbon, and barbeque. Frankly, he spent most of his twenties enjoying the same stuff. As a result, his health suffered. In his midforties, a troubling cardiac health event inspired him to turn his life around. Ken talked to a friend about getting healthier, eating better, and exercising more. His buddy talked him into a couch-to-5K training program, and they partnered up to do an organized race three months away. He liked running so much that the 5Ks turned into 10Ks, half-marathons, and a full marathon within a year. Next, he turned to triathlons, and then, ultimately, the trajectory led to Ken doing an Ironman race: a 2.4-mile swim, 112-mile bike, and 26.2-mile run. Because of his charity work during his earlier marathon and triathlon seasons, one of the charities gave him a bib number for Kona, the world-class triathlon, which is known as the toughest sporting event on the planet. Ken knew training for and completing this race was related to what he cared about—taking care of his health and contributing to charitable endeavors—and he wanted to make sure that he'd be doing his best to prepare for this experience.

He hired Shannon, a certified personal trainer, to help him prepare for the herculean endurance event. They discussed proper nutrition, hydration, and supplementation, along with plans for adequate rest, massage, and stretching to help his body grow fitter and more prepared for this challenge. Of course, the biggest part of their discussions was about physical training. Shannon developed steps for training—swimming, biking, running, and gym workouts for each day of the week, with a day of rest and recovery, of course. She also introduced him to meditation exercises, even though he was skeptical about how they were linked to his training. All the details of these workouts were printed on a two-page training plan, but these summaries were written on his MAP, and then connected to his values with respect to health and fitness:

Doing	To-Do List		
	50 min., 2000m Swim workout, Monday	65 min. 2000m Swim Tempo workout, Friday	
	45 min. Bike workout, Tuesday	3 hr. 15 min. Bike workout, Saturday	
	Full *rest* day, Wednesday (seriously!)	90 min. Run, Zone 1 and 2, Sunday	
	45 min. Run, 3x6 Zone 2 w/ 2 min. recoveries in Zone 1, Thursday	20 min. meditation exercise every day!	
		Follow nutrition guide every day!	

Choosing What Steps to Take

When you clarify your values and articulate your goals, you can create a solid to-do list to direct your action. Your list will differ from Ken's list, even if you have similar values related to your own health and well-being. In chapter 3, you were asked to write your current, specific, observable goals, and also the goals that you'd like to aim for in your life. When it's time to engage in those actions mindfully, fill in the Doing section (the To-Do List) of your MAP with the necessary steps you have to take to complete those commitments, just like Ken did with this different group of tasks.

Alternately, you may have identified valued qualities of actions that are less concrete—perhaps "self-respect," "willingness to be vulnerable," or "generosity." These values may or may not cross many domains. You could begin by picking a domain (perhaps one that you feel a bit lost or stuck in), and thinking about what goals or actions in that domain would serve this purpose, what in your life needs to change for you to practice this value more often, and what specific goals you could aim for in light of that. If a value is "generosity," you might think of ways to contribute more to your community (such as volunteering for a cause that is aligned with other values), or within your relationships (such as considering how you might help a friend), or in the way you work (such as taking on an unpaid but important task like volunteering at a conference).

Ultimately, the MAP helps you figure out what to do to live in service of what you care about, and then to follow through on those actions. The key is that the actions you choose for the Doing section of your MAP are measurable—that is, you can check them off as being "done" and know that you're moving in the direction of your values.

You can approach creating a doing list from a few different directions. As just suggested, you can start with thinking about how you might move in the direction of the values you've identified so far—what actions can you do along the way? Just brainstorm a list of what you *could* do that seems in line with these values.

You can also approach this from the other direction, as you did in the last chapter when you connected your values to the activities that you do too much or too little of. Do that again now with your current to-do list. Can you identify the values these actions might relate to? Try sorting your planned actions into the valued domains of living on your Life Atlas.

When you've finished brainstorming and categorizing, pick a few actions you'd like to engage in that are in service of what you care about. Note them here:

Value: _____

Actions: _____

_____

_____

_____

Value: _____

Actions: _____

_____

_____

_____

Value: _____

Actions: _____

_____

_____

_____

Take a moment to reflect on your new to-do list. Be curious and pay attention to how it feels when you link actions to values. Can you adopt an attitude of "I *get* to do these things" because they are related to a life well lived rather than "I *have* to do these things"? Recall, you can say, "I am doing…what I care about!"

In the last chapter, you learned the difference between goals and values: goals are activities and accomplishments that you can check off when you've completed them, and values provide direction and motivation for such actions. You've also made notes about broad, big-picture goals: what you want to accomplish in life in each domain. Some of the actions that you identified above might also be thought of as goals—can any of them be broken into smaller steps? When you look at them, can you immediately see yourself doing them, or do you think you might not know where to start? Some of Ella's actions in the last chapter related to her graduating from college. This big task isn't the kind of item to put as a "to do" in the Doing section of your MAP, but goals like this are really important to identify and articulate. If you want, you can write an overarching goal at the top of the Doing section of your MAP. This can act as a title for your to-do list, but understand that it won't be checked off; it just helps you keep focused on the big picture. Ella would need to write down smaller, executable goals related to "Graduating from College." Similarly, Ken could put "Complete Kona" as the title of his Doing section, and list all the workout actions for the week underneath.

Not all actions need to be in the service of some bigger-picture goal, so long as they're measurable themselves. If you know that you feel better (i.e., your actions are aligned with your values around health and well-being) when you have a regular morning routine that includes some quiet time to yourself and a walk around the block, your goal may simply be to do that regularly. You almost certainly have some bigger-picture goals, though, or you wouldn't be reading this book! Return to the list of goals you've already identified, along with the list of actions above, and then categorize those bigger-picture goals that you have as well as specific actions you know you might want to do as being in service of your identified values.

Value: _____

Goal: _____

_____

_____

Actions: _____

_____

_____

Value: _____

Goal: _____

_____

_____

Actions: _____

_____

_____

Value: _____

Goal: _____

_____

_____

Actions: _____

_____

_____

Linking Actions to SMARTER and WISE Goals

Now that you're a little clearer about your goals, it's time to optimize them. You may have read about "SMART" goals, but we suggest making "SMARTER" goals. The SMART acronym has been defined in many ways, but we'll use the definition developed by Graham Yemm (2013): goals should **S**pecific, **M**easurable, **A**chievable, **R**elevant, **T**ime-bound, **E**valuated, and **R**ewarded:

- **Specific:** Define or "pinpoint" an explicit description of what you'll be doing. Make the goal precise so that you know when you're working on it and when you aren't.

- **Measurable:** Quantify what's going to be done—that is, how will you know you've done it? If possible, describe the goal with how often (e.g., three days a week, daily) or how long (e.g., twenty minutes, two hours) you're going to engage in this activity.

- **Achievable:** Clarify that the goal is within your capabilities and control, and that you understand your limitations. You can still try to overcome your limits by using the MAP, but be sure that the action is actually something you have the capacity to achieve. For instance, don't start off with a goal of doing the Kona unless you've done other triathlons already!

- **Relevant:** Does the goal meaningfully contribute to what you care about? Ensure that the goal is related to your valued directions.

- **Time-bound:** Set manageable deadlines to create a sense of urgency. Consider breaking big tasks into smaller ones so that you can do them individually and eventually the whole task will be achieved.

- **Evaluated:** At the deadline you set (see Time-bound above), observe your progress, using the measures you specified for your goal.

- **Rewarded:** Plan a reward for meeting your objective. Sure, it's nice to finish a valued action as its own reward, but it's also nice to celebrate when a big step has been completed!

Not only do we endorse SMARTER goals, but we also strongly suggest WISE goals, meaning: what I'm super excited about, or what I'm significantly enthralled with, or what I'm sincerely engaged in. Any way that you define it, WISE goals are about linking what you care about to doing your actions.

Ultimately, your values help you stay excited, enthralled, or engaged in the committed actions that, in turn, take you toward your valued goals. The differences between these terms are nuanced, but there are distinctions. "Excited" means that it gives a desired emotion and you get an energized thrill by doing the action. "Enthralled" means that it fascinates you or grips your attention, and you're engrossed in the topic, but perhaps not excited about it. "Engaged" means that it interlocks with what's important in your life, and you occupy your time meaningfully, but it doesn't necessarily enthrall or excite you. Remember how we said earlier that values can change how you feel about doing something? That's what we're getting at here.

For example, when Ken thought about completing the Kona, he not only was creating SMARTER goals with Shannon, but also WISE goals. He was inspired to start training because he aimed for better cardiovascular health due to his heart attack scare, but there were other things he chose from his values list, such as charity and self-discipline. He wrote these values in his What I Care About section of the MAP; he could also label them: What I'm Sincerely Engaged In.

The MAP promotes keeping WISE goals in mind as you write out your SMARTER to-do list. Some will be exciting, others enthralling, and many will simply be what you engage in because they're important to a life well lived. While we might like to live life on full-tilt and charge after peak experiences, sometimes we must pack our luggage before the trip and do the laundry after we return. Having a life well lived will require a harmony of exciting, enthralling, and engaging actions, and the MAP will help keep you on such a path.

Take a moment now to revisit at least one of the goals you wrote above. Adjust it as much as necessary to ensure it is both SMARTER and WISE. Write the new version below.

_____

_____

_____

_____

Prioritizing What You Are Doing

Now that you have identified both actions and your goals in a WISE and SMARTER way, it's time to figure out which of these to put on your To-Do List in the Doing section of your MAP. This probably isn't easy, because you likely have many values and many goals, and each one of them will have many potential committed actions. Even though it's not easy, it's important for your journey, so let's try it now. Consider one of the goals you wrote down above—perhaps a goal in a valued domain that you've been feeling a bit lost in. For that goal, write up to ten action steps that could help you achieve that goal. You can draw these from the actions you already identified, or take some time now to break down the goal further.

Goal: _____

Steps that could help me achieve it: _____

_____

_____

_____

_____

_____

_____

_____

_____

_____

To put particular committed actions on the MAP, prioritize what needs to be done first. Consider that list you just created. Which action you choose to do first is a matter of your own perspective, but, as you choose, it helps to keep three things in mind: (1) the urgency-importance ratio, (2) sequence factors, and (3) return on investment. Let's look at all three.

The Urgency-Importance Ratio

The urgency-importance ratio, which we often call the "decision matrix," helps you figure out which committed actions would be best to do first. In the urgency-importance guide below, you'll see two variables: important or urgent. Importance is determined by how closely a particular action links to your values, and urgency has to do with how time-bound the objective is. The variables, when parceled out across the four cells in the chart, give you four quadrants:

The Urgency-Importance Ratio Guide

	Urgent	Not Urgent
Important	Quadrant 1 *Values-based priorities*	Quadrant 2 *Values-based choices*
Not Important	Quadrant 3 *Priorities distantly linked to values*	Quadrant 4 *Trivial matters*

- **Quadrant 1: Important and urgent.** This quadrant is for your values-based priorities. Items here have probably been on your to-do list for a while, and you've been chipping away at them. You likely believe they deserve mindful action *now*.

- **Quadrant 2: Important but not urgent.** This quadrant is for items that are values-based choices, meaning they're important but not urgent. For example, it's usually not urgent that you do loving sweet-nothings for your significant other, but it's sure important to the health of the relationship.

- **Quadrant 3: Not important but urgent.** This quadrant contains urgent items of low importance that still take up your time. You have to make them a priority given their time-based nature, but they're only distantly linked to your values. Spending time in a meeting that could have been handled in an email is a good example.

- **Quadrant 4: Not important or urgent.** This quadrant contains activities that are neither values-based nor time-bound. This quadrant isn't necessarily worthless, but these activities aren't ones likely to make it to a Mindful Action Plan.

Using the urgency-importance ratio guide might not be necessary for everyone, but it's helpful when you're deciding which set of potential committed actions you'd like to prioritize. For example, Ken was swamped with things to do while training, and he had to prioritize what he'd choose to do with respect to importance and urgency. Given the way Shannon set up the training program, Ken needed the discipline (which will get aided with the other areas of the MAP) to put all her coaching exercises in quadrant 1. They were values-based priorities—important to maintaining his health, growth, well-being, and accomplishment—and time-bound insofar as if he skipped even a day, it would significantly diminish his fitness while preparing for the Ironman. He also had tasks related to raising more charity money for this race and he put them in quadrant 2. These tasks sometimes made it to his daily MAP to-do list. While these tasks were important, they weren't urgent, so he did the work regularly but didn't prioritize it above training. Ken also belonged to the board of directors for his condominium association, so he put urgent requests from that group in third place on quadrant 3. He needed to get them done in a judicious manner, but they didn't play a large role in his long-term values. Finally, and unfortunately, much of his time was consumed with scrolling through social media, and this quadrant 4 action never made it to his Mindful Action Plan. Thus, the time he spent on these tasks dwindled because he was linking what he truly cared about (his values) with what he was doing (his committed actions).

EXERCISE: Declaring the Important and Urgent

Take a moment now to apply the urgency-importance ratio to at least one set of committed actions you've identified.

THE URGENCY-IMPORTANCE RATIO GUIDE

	Urgent	Not Urgent
Important	Quadrant 1	Quadrant 2
Not Important	Quadrant 3	Quadrant 4

Sequence Factors

Sometimes the reason for doing one thing before the other is very simple, although we sometimes miss it: it just makes logical sense to go in order. Some processes require a certain order, and organizing them correctly helps to make sure you don't have to backtrack, engage in redundancies, or get bottlenecked with too many things going on at once. You can't set a goal to write a term paper without having met other goals, such as reading the textbooks, reviewing your notes, and attending the classes. Similarly, you can't set a goal to get a new job without preparing your résumé, searching job postings, and reconsidering what you want to do in your career. You can put those overarching goals as titles to your to-do list, but make sure the path to get there goes in an optimal sequential order. When engaging in mindful action, it's clearly helpful to prioritize the temporal order of things, but be judicious about this aim. For example, Ken's to-do list had to include a "rest day" only after he completed the taxing workouts from the days before.

Would any of your actions benefit from being completed in a particular sequence? If so, take the time now to order and prioritize them, identifying the steps to take for this goal and then putting them in the appropriate sequential order to optimize the outcome.

_____

_____

_____

_____

_____

_____

_____

Return on Investment (ROI)

ROI is a popular abbreviation in the finance world, and it makes sense to consider it when planning a life well lived. In other words, when you're choosing what to do mindfully, it makes sense to consider what time, effort, and assets you'll be investing in the action. What's the ratio between your resources expended and the outcome? This is a bit different from the urgency-importance ratio. For instance, maybe you have two goals that are meant to serve, respectively, your values of your health and being a good partner to your significant other. You could declare that the values of your own health and your own intimate relationship are equally important. Because you must work late, you only have an hour of free time when you get home. Do you go for a run or hang out with your significant other? As you read this, you might jump right into one choice and see it as a no-brainer. Maybe you immediately reacted with "Hang out with my S.O.!" But what if you've been doing that so much this month that your health is deteriorating, and you're missing out on your favorite hobby? Those unhealthy consequences can also tear at the fabric of a relationship. On the other hand, maybe you immediately reacted with "Go for a run!" But what if your partner truly needs you to sit with them and have a stress-reducing conversation tonight? Coming up with what to do can be a daily challenge, and we're tested to find that harmony between the different things we value. Frankly, it might just be a good idea for some couples to exercise together!

Look at your goals, or at least one of the goals that you've been struggling with, and reflect for a moment: If you invested in this action right here and now, what valued outcomes would you experience? What gives you the best ROI? Take a moment to note this now.

Thinking about all your goals and committed actions in these ways helps you determine what to do first, and how to prioritize committed actions on your to-do list.

Flexible Prioritizing

Importantly, the Mindful Action Plan helps you recognize the external cultural push to conform socially, which can sometimes lead to doing—but doing things you don't truly care about. It's possible to misinterpret this chapter and think you have to be doing the "right" things and doing them "rightly!" Remember, there's no single behavior that's "right" or "wrong." The only consideration is the function a particular behavior serves in *your* life, and whether that behavior is effective for you or not in light of the particular outcomes you might want at any given time. The standard for doing things right is set by what you care about—and what you care about at any given time can change.

Also, the question of whether what you're doing is in line with what you care about is one that's up to you to answer. The sections of this chapter about getting things done and optimizing performance are still worthy, because they'll help you choose to do things that you truly value, and do them in a way that meets your standards. At the same time, we have to accept both that there are behaviors and ways of living your life that are less effective *and* that, on a fundamental level, there's nothing "wrong" with the way you're living your life. Ultimately, there's no wrong way for a life well lived. Your life is yours to live. So as you work on your to-do list, using the guidelines throughout this chapter, remember that, when it comes to figuring out what you want to do to make your goals and values a reality, you can't make a mistake.

Arranging Your External World for Your To-Do List

Recall that doing is where the rubber hits the road with the MAP. Sure, having a to-do list helps your productivity, but just putting these tasks on a sheet of paper isn't the only way to get traction and move forward. This is why the MAP put a "gas tank" at the bottom of the checklist—Designing Success with Performance Management—and it's up to you to fill 'er up with a workable incentive plan to help you actually take the steps you've written out. Performance management, a well-established intervention for improving productivity that has been around for decades, helps you utilize the power of applied behavioral sciences by guiding you to consider three ABCs of human performance: antecedents (A), behaviors (B), and consequences (C). Consultants, coaches, and clinicians who work with changing people's habits start by defining the behavior (B) the person wants to see more or less of, then they analyze the antecedents (A) that come before it and the consequences (C) that come after it. Analyzing the surrounding environment to a behavior is very helpful.

You've chosen and defined your behaviors for the to-do list. These are the specific steps you'll take to achieve a particular valued goal you've identified and thereby live a more valued life. Now it's time to *do* them, but there are often external obstacles that prevent you from getting right to it. You started to identify some of these in chapter 3, so let's now take a gander at what the MAP suggests for designing success.

Designing Success with Performance Management	
Make sure all required resources for successful actions have been acquired.	
Publicly announce your commitment to meet performance goals.	
Alert your accountability partner about your commitment and goals.	
Describe incentives, performance criteria, and deadlines:	

Make Sure All Required Resources for Successful Actions Have Been Acquired

Basically, the heading of this section encourages you to control many of the antecedents necessary for the chosen behavior. Do you have the knowledge, environmental support, and tools for the job? It's a lot simpler to engage in doing what you care about when you have the resources. For instance, DJ was working on his dissertation in the 1990s—prior to every household having a home computer—and was not very productive with his writing. He had to drive fifteen miles to the campus computer lab whenever he needed to write, which severely cut into time available to work on his research. When he finally acquired a laptop, a "required resource" for him, he made real progress on writing his dissertation. For Ken's required resources, he (with Shannon's help) identified technical gear like specific swim and cycling equipment, and better shoes that he acquired before he started training.

When you look at your own to-do list, what antecedents (or "things that come before the behavior") need to be acquired to make this work? Do you need specific equipment (whether that's a sharp pencil, a computer, or a bathing suit)? Do you need to buy a book, meet with your boss, sign up for a class, get your car fixed, or make an appointment with a doctor, counselor, or other professional to help you? Write some of those items in the section below to help you familiarize yourself with the process of anticipating your own antecedents for any to-do lists that you might fashion for yourself as you continue to use the MAP.

We're not implying that you need to have everything perfectly in order before you begin to work on a goal. Many successful people didn't have the optimum resources when they began their journey. You can imagine a boxer who has no gloves, no coach, and no punching bag, but they run, skip rope, shadowbox, and drink raw eggs (high-five to the *Rocky* fans), until they develop enough skill and fitness to catch someone's eye—someone who'll take a chance on them. Conversely, we want to warn you against "pencil sharpening," a term for a particular procrastination technique in which an author, for instance, behaves as though they must have everything they'll need in place before they start to write. Because they can never have *everything* in place, they avoid writing and, with it, the risk of failure. Sure, the sequential order of having a sharpened pencil first before writing down your ideas makes a lot of sense, but sharpening ten pencils is just avoiding the task.

Look again at the actions that you've identified in the Doing and What I Care About sections of your MAP, and then generate a list of things that can help you get started on these effectively. If you want to design success, make sure you have the tools and training *to do* what you value.

To-do list item: _____

What antecedents do I need to achieve this?

_____

_____

To-do list item: _____

What antecedents do I need to achieve this?

_____

_____

To-do list item: _____

What antecedents do I need to achieve this?

_____

_____

Publicly Announce Your Commitment to Meet Performance Goals

Oftentimes, it's a good idea to tell your friends, family, or work associates what your goals are. By doing this, you let people know that you're focused on some important tasks that might take you away from what they might expect of you. Hopefully, it will lead to people cheering you on and asking, "How's it going with your plans?" If you think you'd benefit from this kind of support, then telling others is a good idea. Clearly, we sometimes have objectives that we want to keep private. There are also situations where you know people will be less supportive, tease you about the plans, or perhaps even attempt to dissuade or prevent you from moving forward. Be judicious when building a support team. For instance, Ken's social group was very aware of his aim to run Kona—if you've ever been around a training triathlete, they talk about it all the time! Having their support was exceptionally important in helping Ken stick to his training.

Take a moment now and consider in what context it would be helpful to you to make a public commitment to at least one of your goals (or as many as you like).

Goal: _____

How will I publicly commit to this?

_____

_____

Goal: _____

How will I publicly commit to this? _____

_____

_____

Goal: _____

How will I publicly commit to this? _____

_____

_____

Alert Your Accountability Partner About Your Commitment and Goals

While telling many people about your plan for mindful action may be a good idea (but with some potential downsides), choosing a single accountability partner definitely increases your chances for engaging in a higher rate of committed actions! A close friend or even someone a bit further from your inner circle could be a good accountability partner. As the African proverb says, "If you want to go fast, go alone; if you want to go far, go together." You do committed actions alone, but if you want to reach certain goals further in the distance, having an accountability partner to support you is key. The MAP harmonizes these choices.

Choosing a person (or several if you have separate goals that you want to keep private) holds you accountable to the contingencies you set for yourself. Research clearly shows that people aren't good at providing their own consequences (Hayes, Zettle, and Rosenfarb 1989), so asking a trusted person to help would be a good idea! The bottom part of the MAP where you describe your personal incentives also has a place to collaborate with your partner on performance criteria and deadlines—a contract with your partner to do the behaviors you say you will.

Shannon, for example, was Ken's critical accountability partner. They collaborated on how she would help him meet his performance criteria by agreed upon deadlines (see below). Who could be your accountability partners? Write down the names of some folks you might trust to be your accountability partners or with whom you could share the goals and valued directions you're setting for yourself. Also note people you'd rather *not* trust with your goals and committed actions, just so you can clarify this for yourself.

_____

_____

_____

_____

_____

_____

Describe Incentives, Performance Criteria, and Deadlines

In the Designing Success with Performance Management section of the MAP, you and your accountability partner will develop the carrot-and-stick routine for your actions. Some performance coaches call this "contingency management." This means you develop if-then statements that set up particular consequences for particular behaviors that will motivate you: *if* you meet certain objectives, *then* good stuff will happen, and *if* you do not hit the marks, *then* some crummy stuff occurs. Ken identified some of his sports gear as necessary resources (antecedents), but Shannon also wanted to use some other gear as consequences, or rewards for completing certain actions week after week. Ken kept telling her that he wanted fancy socks to go with his high-tech equipment, so she wrote a behavioral contract on the bottom of the MAP to help Ken commit more fully to what he would be doing for training:

Designing Success with Performance Management	
Make sure all required resources for successful actions have been acquired.	X
Publicly announce your commitment to meet performance goals.	X
Alert your accountability partner about your commitment and goals.	X
Describe incentives performance criteria, and deadlines:	
If I complete every workout in this week's Doing list, do the meditations, and follow the nutrition guide appropriately, I can purchase my fancy socks on Sunday evening.	

Think about this section of your MAP in the context of some of the actions you've been struggling to get done. For example, you value health and well-being, and you put "call my physician for a checkup" on your To-Do List in the Doing section of the MAP. However, if you've been putting off actually doing it for weeks, then you might benefit from a contingency plan like this: "If I make my doctor's appointment by 5:00 p.m. tonight, then I get to watch an hour of TV tonight. If I do not meet this criterion by that deadline, then I'll send five dollars to my ex's favorite charity." Maybe you don't have a TV or an ex (or they don't have a favorite charity), or maybe five dollars is a pittance to you. The point is to create your own performance management contract. See if you can embrace the tactile pen-and-paper approach of this to-do list. Consider this specific way of organizing your behavior as a welcomed discipline and an improvement from writing your to-dos on a sticky note or the back of a used envelope.

Moving Forward

This chapter discussed doing what you care about: coming up with goals that'll help you put your values into practice, and figuring out the specific steps that will help you achieve those goals. You're beginning to find your *way*.

As you use the MAP, we encourage you to engage in ongoing, active reflection on what you've been doing and getting done. What valued domains of your life are getting more or less attention? What isn't getting done? Return to the performance management section of the MAP and consider how you might rearrange your environment to make it more likely that you'll get these important and meaningful tasks done. For instance, Ken chose to put his running shoes by his bed instead of by the front door of his house so he'd be ready to run before he left his bedroom. He also kept his smartphone away from his bed so he'd be less likely to scroll social media during the morning hour when he could be running.

Consider whether the values you identified as being relevant are really personally important. With these tasks and values in mind, you might return to chapter 4 and reflect on the exercises there. Or perhaps other barriers are presenting themselves in your internal world; the remaining chapters of this book will help you with that! For example, Ken needed to work on more than just committing to valued actions. He also had to work with some hard emotions and thoughts—like his fear of possibly failing at a deeply important task. To help with this, Shannon worked with him to customize his MAP phrase: "I am here now, accepting my feelings of anxiety, noticing my thoughts that I might fail, while training well to take care of my health and provide for charitable endeavors."

In the next four chapters, we'll explore more deeply how the MAP phrase sets a context for maintaining valued commitments. Let's begin with a deeper dive into mindfulness from the MAP perspective.

CHAPTER 6

Here Now

The MAP focuses on committed *action*—doing what you care about—which we focused on in the last few chapters. Yet, if it were enough to simply write down your goals, break them down into actions, connect them to your values, and create performance management contracts for yourself, you probably wouldn't have picked up this book in the first place. You'd just be successfully doing all the stuff that's important to you without any concerns. However, you probably don't check everything off your to-do list, no matter how well you plan. At times, you may even feel that it's impossible to take the next step forward. That's where the remaining sections of the MAP come in. Once you've found your *why* and begun to identify where you are on your path and what the next steps need to be, you'll need to learn new skills and strategies. You'll need some wayfinding tools for staying on your path, taking steps forward, and continually getting your bearings. You'll determine if you've gotten stuck, turned around, or gone on an unplanned detour—and then figure out how to get back on track. In this chapter and the following three chapters, we'll identify how we create our own obstacles to valued actions and practice strategies for working with those hindrances. In this chapter, we focus on being in the here and now while engaging in our Mindful Action Plan.

One major challenge to finding your way and sticking to it is getting sidetracked by traveling back and forth in time—not literally, of course, but by getting caught up in thinking about the past and the future. But *now* is the only time you can behave, and *here* is the only place you can act. To reiterate, the only place and time you can do anything is here now. In acceptance and commitment therapy, we call this skill "contacting the present moment," and on the MAP, it's simply Here Now.

Our definition of mindful action introduced earlier requires such action to be "present-focused." But our minds aren't always focused on here and now. Approximately 47 percent of the day, our thoughts are elsewhere—there and then—instead of here and now (Killingsworth and Gilbert 2010).

For almost half of the day, you're likely to be thinking about things that might happen in the future, have happened in the past, or are happening elsewhere—rather than what you're presently doing here and now. If this seems incredible, look closely at your own experience. When you tell yourself that you're going to be laser focused on a project, doesn't it still take longer than you estimated? And during the time you're working, don't your thoughts meander around other topics rather than focusing exclusively on your task? A wandering mind isn't necessarily problematic in every instance, but it can be! Planning things in the future, reminiscing about the past, and remembering problem solutions can be helpful. Yet, *worrying* about the future and *ruminating* about the past steal the vitality of the present moment and can be problematic. You can probably already identify with this particular obstacle on your path—getting distracted or worried by what's up ahead, or looking back at what you passed by before. As an illustration, let's meet Glen and Kay Tipton, and their son, Ron.

● *The Tiptons' Story*

When little Ron swatted a bowlful of his favorite cereal across the kitchenette, he yelled, "I don't want this!" Glen and Kay looked at each other, bracing for another tantrum. Fortunately, their pediatrician's office held weekly parent management training (PMT) classes to help with these kinds of concerns. After some self-assessment, Glen and Kay recognized one major issue ramping up Ron's tantrums: they simply weren't paying attention to him until his behavior was so problematic that it required their attention. Too often they attended to their smartphone, the game on the TV, or other trivial matters at hand, instead of giving attention to their son when he appropriately requested it. When Ron's wants and needs were unattended, he raised his voice and engaged in problematic behavior to get the attention he sought. When Ron's parents finally reinforced that kind of behavior with their attention, he then began his requests with that level of intensity. One of the things the PMT educator suggested was "catch him being good" or, in other words, reinforce the child when his behavior is appropriate for the situation so tantrums aren't necessary for parental attention. This is good advice from the pediatric professionals, but the catch is that quite often Glen and Kay were there and then instead of being here and now.

Ron's mom and dad didn't have to work hard to find their why for changing their behavior. On the parenting part of their Life Atlas, each had stated, "Rearing Ron to live a full, healthy, enjoyable life." Their valued direction didn't include allowing Ron to grow up with a treatable childhood behavior disorder, so Glen and Kay realized they needed to find their way not only by doing the skills their parent training suggested, but also by contacting the present moment more often when around their child.

Here Now: The Time and Place for *Mindful* Action

Like Glen and Kay, if you truly want to do what you care about in your life—fully committed to engaging in valued actions—then building skills to focus on being here now is critical. "Life is the duration of one breath," according to the Buddha. No matter what your spiritual beliefs, does that phrase resonate with you? Life is experienced in the present moment. Of course, you could argue that the duration of life is from the first breath to the last breath, but that's just another use of the word "life." You can also view the duration of life as the experience from this breath to this breath. If you're struggling with the difference, it's just a matter of perspective on the definition of life. One way looks at the biological measure from birth to death, and the other is the experiential measure from now to now.

If you're not regularly focused on the here and now, and are frequently caught up in thoughts about there and then, you'll be distracted, drawn away from your plans, and governed by things that have little to do with your valued behavior. Mindful action planning thus aims to help you not only to *be* more mindful but also to *act* more mindfully. One might argue that mindfulness isn't about goal-directed striving, but at the same time, mindfulness is not just about time spent in lotus position on a cushion either. The point of the MAP isn't to optimize how long or how well you can meditate, but instead to sustain your commitment to what you care about doing in this moment. When you invest time and effort into building mindful*ness* skills to assist you to be in the here and now, you'll be able to apply powerful mindful action to improve your valued journey.

A Piece of the MAP: Here Now

| Here Now | Center your situational awareness on what you are doing. Contact what is happening here and now. Rather than getting wrapped up in events not in your present control, let go of these distracting events. Focus on what is relevant to your actions. | |

This section of the MAP helps you contact the present moment so you can be aware of opportunities to engage in meaningful behavior. Mindful action can be promoted with repeated practice: center your situational awareness on what you're doing, notice what's happening here and now, and then, rather than getting wrapped up in events not in your present control, let go of distracting events and stay focused on what's relevant to your actions. We'll unpack this section of the MAP throughout the chapter. Let's begin simply with the experience of what it feels like to be here now—choosing a behavior and sensing how the action is being performed in the present moment.

Exercise: A Simple Mindful Action

The MAP asks you to "center your situational awareness on what you are doing"—that is, to focus on your *action* in this present moment. To learn this skill, let's do a very simple mindfulness exercise, right here and now. As you follow these directions, observe that you are in contact with the present moment as you do so.

> Focus on resting your tongue gently on the roof of your mouth about a half an inch away from your front teeth. If you typically have good posture, your tongue might already be there. For the next few moments, fully practice this proper tongue placement: keep your lips closed and your teeth slightly separated. Right here and now, sense how the tip of your tongue feels. Feel your tongue touching the front part of the roof of your mouth. Gently press your tongue forward. Feel the pressure, here and now. Sense your tongue on your hard palate.

> The sensing, feeling, pressing, and focusing are all things you are doing. They are behaviors being done in the here and now. This extremely simple exercise shows both how your actions happen in the present moment and that you can attend to these actions.

Acting Here Now

You improve your skills for doing what you care about when you're in the here and now, so we strongly encourage you to start doing mindful practices if you aren't already. Both formal, disciplined meditation exercises and informal, deliberate mindfulness micropractices can help with attending to your own actions in the here and now.

Traditional mindfulness exercises provide an established framework for practicing the skills for contacting the present moment. For instance, the classic sitting meditation invites you to simply hold a dignified posture while being aware of your breath as you inhale and exhale. This is an exercise in becoming more skillful at acting here and now. When you do this exercise, if thoughts, images, or sensations show up for you, simply be aware of their presence and gently bring yourself back to your commitment of being aware of your breathing. There are other methods of doing traditional mindfulness exercises, such as gazing at a candle, chanting a mantra, or doing yoga. Having a time-honored method for practicing mindfulness will provide support and direction as you develop your skills for being in the present moment. Doing these practices not only helps you get into a state of mindfulness but also prepares you for mindful action.

Informal mindful micropractices are shorter exercises you can do during your activities of daily living. At different times of the day in various contexts, you can deliberately choose to be aware of your experience of the present moment. You see the sights and hear the sounds in your world, become attuned to your behaviors, and simply bring yourself back to the present if thoughts or judgments arise. Being conscious of the present moment is more likely to happen if you practice it in many different situations—not only in the distraction-free environment you might have when practicing formally but also out in the dynamic world.

Both traditional and informal practices, when done on a regular basis, build up skills to help you more readily contact the present moment. To make an analogy, if you wanted to be an expert basketball player, you'd practice your three-point shots two different ways: (1) go to the gym alone and take shot after shot in a disciplined manner to build better accuracy, and (2) participate in pickup games with other players so that there's distracting activity, vibrant movement, and even opponents trying to block your three-pointer. When you're in the gym alone, you can do specific methodical exercises, and when you're in the game, it's like a real-world practice session. Both traditional meditations and informal micropractices can contribute to your psychological flexibility.

Although this isn't a book on formal mindfulness practices, we certainly encourage them because they can help you to more frequently be present for longer durations. As with exercising your body, the more you exercise your mind, the stronger and more enduring your focus will be. Or, if these kinds of practices just don't speak to you, that's fine too! You don't need a formal meditation practice in order to practice being here now in lots of other ways that can help you stay on your path.

Center Your Situational Awareness

Mindful action is supported by situational awareness skills. *Situational awareness* is "the perception of the elements in the environment within a volume of time and space, the comprehension of their meaning and a projection of their status in the near future" (Endsley et al. 1998). The term "situational awareness" comes from the industrial-organizational psychology literature, and the concept solidly overlaps with contacting the present moment in ACT and Here Now skills in the MAP. The MAP has been used in several industrial-organizational psychology applications, and it seemed prudent to use the term "situational awareness" instead of mindfulness in some scenarios. For example, when DJ first pitched using ACTraining to improve safety behaviors on a construction site, the supervisor ridiculed the idea of teaching mindfulness to the blue-collar workers. He actually said, "I don't think my guys are going to start saying 'Namaste' to each other after the toolbox meetings. We're trying to get the guys to wear their hard hats more often…not trying to get them to start wearing yoga pants. Nobody wants to see my guys in yoga pants!" Knowing that many on the crew had been in the military, and also were more likely to embrace something that sounded more practical, DJ taught the mindfulness practices but called them "situational awareness" exercises to help the workers be more readily in the here and now. ACT is pragmatic at its core, so adjusting terms as needed is helpful.

Situational Awareness Skills Building

When you're doing what you care about, perceiving the elements around you in the here and now, seeing how they relate to your values and goals, and focusing on working on the current objective, you're engaged in mindful action. This is situational awareness. You can begin to expand your situational awareness by noticing what's happening here and now rather than getting wrapped up in events not in your present control. Take some time to read and follow each of these directions, and just notice your environment:

- Find something blue to see.

- Sense the place on your back between your shoulder blades.

- Feel the difference between the coolness of the air as you inhale through your nose, and how it's warmer when you exhale.

- Seek a direction you would go if trouble arose in your surroundings.

- Look for something asymmetrical. Imagine it morphed into something symmetrical.

- Listen to your environment in a way that you hear something you wouldn't have typically focused on, and now focus on listening to it some more.

- Label the emotion that you are feeling right now.

Developing skillful situational awareness benefits your committed actions because when you exercise how you sense the external world and how you relate to your own internal world, you'll more regularly pick up cues for valued action. For instance, when the Tiptons were learning parent management training skills, the educator also incorporated mindfulness training. The couple supported each other when doing the situational awareness exercises, and they started seeing the practical benefit of the practice because they were becoming more alert to Ron when he needed attention. They found themselves parenting their son in the here and now rather than focusing on their social media page or the TV. For the Tiptons, following through on valued behavior in the here and now was overwhelmingly more important than those distracting trivialities, which were "not urgent and not important" activities—that is, activities that they didn't want to prioritize.

When you're situationally aware of your external surroundings, you do what you care about more readily by building a supportive context for living a life of meaning and purpose. You'll see if you have the resources you need and the support you want, and you'll also perceive the obstacles that may impede doing what you care about and react accordingly. In addition, once you're situationally aware of your internal world (your emotions, sensations, and mood states), you begin to accept what you feel. You'll label your emotions so you can connect them to the way you have successfully—or unsuccessfully—dealt with them in similar situations. This facilitates strategies for effective valuable action in the current moment.

EXERCISE: Contact the Present Emotion

ACT invites you to contact the present moment with mindfulness exercises. You've likely been introduced to exercises where you attend to your breath, and we'll expand on that with a bit of a twist. We invite you to toggle back and forth between your internal and external world.

> Inhale slowly, and notice the coolness of the breath. Gently hold that breath and look away from reading this text for a moment to notice an object in your external world, and then come back to the text.

> Now exhale slowly and notice the warmth of this breath. Inhale again, notice the coolness compared to the exhale, and hold it again. Find that object again, and contact the fact that there's something external to you that you can experience here and now. Exhale slowly, and sense the warmth, and contact the fact that there's something internal you're experiencing here and now.

You toggled back and forth between things you can sense within your body and outside your body. Now let's go deeper.

> Sense your emotion. In this present moment, contact a feeling. Perhaps you're feeling content, curious, bored, confused, or some other emotion. Simply use the same perspective you had

when you were observing that external object, and observe this feeling. It is present, and it isn't you…it is in the context of you, right here and right now. Emotions are regularly there within you, and you can focus on them and be aware of your internal world.

Now, look at that object in the external world. This, too, is something that you can center your situational awareness on here and now. Toggle back and forth with your attention between the external and the internal a few more times.

And now, embrace this perspective: you and the world are a unitary whole. The way you feel is often influenced by the world around you, and the world around you gets affected by the way you feel. Observe the connection of your external and internal world. Observe with situational awareness that you are one with the world…here and now.

When doing such a skills-building exercise, you're learning that you can be aware of the experiences at your disposal that will play a role in your actions. Reliably being in the here and now promotes awareness of how you feel, what you're thinking, who you identify as, and also what's going on in the world around you. All of these processes and outcomes support your values-based committed actions.

Now look at your Life Atlas, and then your MAP, and focus on the part where you're Doing What I Care About. How would being situationally aware be helpful to your actions?

_____

_____

_____

Letting Go of Distracting Events

We're still unpacking the directions from the Mindful Action Plan, and being here now requires letting go of distracting events, and this can be a difficult task! When you were doing some of the above exercises, such as aiming to "find something blue to see," you may have noticed yourself talking to yourself about the experience. If you were doing this exercise outside on a cloudless day, and had already admired the sky earlier, your mind probably just said something like *That's easy. Just look up!* Language can be very helpful that way. But maybe you're reading this while sitting in the library with your legs under a desk. This is a new place for you to read, so nothing quickly comes to mind to complete this challenge of finding something blue to see. Your mind starts groping, *There's probably a book on the shelf over there with a blue binding,* and when you don't see one, your mind thinks, *No?! Hmm. I'm surprised. The whole shelf and not a single blue binding. That's weird. Blue is a popular color, isn't it? I mean...especially for books! I can't believe I can't find a blue thing, especially in a library. Sheesh...there's even something called the* Blue Book. *Well, that book wouldn't be on the shelf here because that's for car buying. And I should probably find that publication because my car has been giving me trouble...* And the whole time your mind was thinking about these things that have relatively nothing to do with your task, you were wearing denim jeans! You could have found something blue fairly quickly if you'd kept engaged in a committed action of looking for it, but your thoughts acted as an obstacle, presenting you with all kinds of distracting events. Now think about how you sometimes work on much more important tasks than finding something blue, and how your thoughts are obstacles to your valued committed actions.

So far in this chapter, you've been practicing the first two steps of learning to engage in more mindful action—centering your situational awareness on what you're doing (and experiencing) and contacting how that action feels. The next step is to "let go of" distracting thoughts not in service to your committed actions that you're doing here and now—that is, you can learn to relate to those distracting events differently; just because you're thinking something doesn't mean it has to govern your time and efforts. You just read a silly example of mindlessness about getting caught up in stray thoughts about needing to replace your car while looking for something blue, even though you're currently wearing blue jeans. On the other hand, getting caught up in your thoughts like this can be intensely problematic when you commit to a valued action, and you aren't in the here and now but rather there and then—and therefore you're not acting optimally or even acting at all! For example, consider an author with a deadline, and they ruminate so long about how bad a writer they are that they don't finish their manuscript on time. Or when a dad, who values good parenting, is asked to volunteer for a necessary task for the school play, and instead of saying yes to the request, he worries about all the things that could go wrong and how inconvenienced he would be if he does what he's asked to do. Consider the Tiptons. They truly love their son, Ron, but instead of interacting with him in the here and now, they sometimes get caught up with things they really don't value but that are immediately gratifying, like odd videos their friends post on social media—that is, they get caught up in the there and then. If folks can let go of their urges, thoughts, and emotions, look at them from a distance, and clarify what is valuable and meaningful, then important committed actions would be more successfully accomplished in the present moment. This is a life well lived.

Your Distracting Events

As mentioned earlier, people spend 47 percent of the day thinking about there and then instead of here and now. Mindlessness happens to everyone, so how is it going to happen to you when you're busy with your valued commitments? There are myriad ways that you get distracted, but we invite you to take a look at the goals you generated for the Doing section in the MAP, and predict what kinds of thoughts about there and then will pop up while you're in the here and now engaging in valued committed action. It's bound to happen, so see if you can articulate now what to look out for while you're engaged in doing what you care about. Write down what you guess you might be distracted by and that you would do well to let go of.

Action: _____

Distraction: _____

_____

_____

_____

Action: _____

Distraction: _____

_____

_____

_____

Focusing on Relevant Action

Mindful action is about *maximally attending* to doing what you care about. This is a very jargony portion of the mindful action definition, but we really want to make this point. *Maximally attending* means that—as much as possible—you'll spend your time and attention on your valued commitments while doing them. You pay maximum attention to the actions that are relevant to your values. The more you build skills for paying attention, the more successful you will be with your commitments. And that's the other thing about the jargon: paying attention seems like an unworthy idiom for what we're doing. We aren't really *paying* anything! As behavioral scientists who are trying to help journeyers with their commitments, we're simply being more exact in what behavior is expected. *Attending* means being present with an event and dealing with it successfully. When you're engaged in mindful action, you're *maximally attending* to your task, or being present and dealing with it successfully for as much time as you can.

Here's one of the main reasons we encourage focusing on your actions: the same research that found that we aren't paying attention to what we're doing for nearly half the day, also tells us that "people were less happy when their minds were wandering than when they were not" (Killingsworth and Gilbert 2010, 932). The MAP aims to help you improve your focus on the important commitments in your life. It encourages you to be in the here and now when you do them and to practice mindfulness skills to assist with that… and it seems like being happier might be a nice side effect for all this effort!

● *The Tiptons' Story*

Since the Tiptons learned that parent management training supported doing what they care about (rearing a healthy child), they chose to dedicate themselves to being more mindful of the here and now so that they wouldn't miss cues for action from Ron. "Our boy is only young once" became the Tiptons' present-focused catchphrase while working on their parenting together, and they put this phrase on their parenting MAP in the Here Now section. This brought them into the current moment, instead of focusing on what parenting "used to be" like and hoping that Ron would soon outgrow this phase. The Tiptons realized they were thinking about there and then more than acting in the here and now. Obviously, Ron's tantrums are annoying and hard to bear, and they are also the reality of the here and now. Wishing them away wouldn't work, and it would probably make the problem worse. They weren't sharing a present moment with their child. Instead of being caught up in there-and-then situations that they couldn't influence, they committed to embracing the moment-by-moment, lovable here and now. With the actions they identified from their parent training, plus their reminder to stay focused on the here now, the Tiptons felt like they were finally making some headway with both teaching their son the skills he needed to thrive, as well as appreciating the path that they were on in this moment of his life. They also created their own MAP phrase: "We are here now, accepting our feelings of annoyance, noticing our thoughts about escaping through looking at TV or our social media, while parenting effectively and being attentive to his needs because we love this little bundle of joy and irritation."

EXERCISE: Sampling Mindful Action Here and Now

The Tiptons successfully started engaging in mindful action, and now it's your turn. This exercise isn't about doing a guided meditation or breathing mindfully, but instead it's about really giving values-based action a go, right here, right now. Look at the goals you came up with that are related to your values, and contact the present moment by taking a simple step in that direction. Truly engage in overt behavior in the service of your chosen values—behavior that is measurable. There are no blank lines under this exercise to write your answers or intentions to do later, because we're inviting you to do what you care about here and now. If you made a commitment to get better at guitar, then pick up your six-string. If you committed to repairing a relationship with an estranged family member, then outline the first letter you will write them. If your values-based behavior is to pick up a meditation practice, then put this book down, get in a comfortable position in your chair, slowly inhale, and close your eyes.

Moving Forward

As noted earlier in the workbook, psychological flexibility involves mindful action. In this chapter, you began the journey of acting with full awareness of what you're doing, aiming to be more reliably in the here and now while engaged in valued actions, spending most of your attention on the stuff you choose to be important in your life, and creating a context supporting the practice of mindfulness. The chapter guided you through the here now concepts of mindful action. Over the course of the next three chapters, you'll learn even more skills for keeping your attention focused on what's important rather than being distracted by the obstacles your own thoughts place on your path.

CHAPTER 7

Accepting

Now that you've practiced being more reliably in the here and now, let's attend to another obstacle to mindful action: your emotions. While you focused on contacting the present moment, perhaps you found yourself caught up in how you were feeling and had difficulty attending to the here and now. Emotions exert strong influence over thoughts and actions, and not only can they take you out of the current moment, but they can also impede valued action.

Reflecting on your experience, can you recall a time when your emotions had a significant impact on doing important actions? How have your feelings influenced you to act in a psychologically inflexible manner? Think back to the exercise of building your Life Atlas. Did any of your own feelings show up and act as an obstacle for choosing what's important to you? Building the skill of accepting your emotions will have a powerful influence on your ability to keep commitments to your value-based actions.

A Piece of the MAP: Accepting

| Accepting | Allow yourself to acknowledge any emotions you are having without trying to control the emotions. Be willing to simply have those feelings while moving forward with valuable actions. | |

This section of the MAP promotes skills related to increasing your willingness to experience your feelings in a healthy manner so you can be open to opportunities for engaging in meaningful behavior. Sometimes challenging emotions will arise *because* you're engaging in values-based actions, and accepting sets a context to allow those feelings to be present without them impeding your journey forward. Mindful action is supported when you allow yourself to acknowledge any emotions you're having without trying to control them. The Accepting section on the MAP encourages you to be willing to simply have your feelings while moving forward with valued actions. This is, of course, much easier said than done. In this chapter, we'll look at what makes it difficult to accept (rather than trying to change) many emotions, sensations, urges, and other feelings, and learn strategies for making space for these internal experiences to be part of our journey. "Acceptance" is a core skill in acceptance and commitment therapy—it is, after all, part of the name!—and that's what we'll focus on now as a core component of the MAP.

The Basic Problem: Control

If you're *not* doing what you care about, perhaps something about this action is emotionally difficult for you. When faced with aversive situations—in other words, anything that is unpleasant, difficult, painful, or otherwise presents events that we do not want to be faced with—we tend to do one of three things: we try to escape, do other things to avoid the situation in the first place, or engage in aggression toward what we perceive as the source of adversity. Fundamentally, we try to *control* the experience we encounter. In our evolutionary history, there were aversive situations in which these methods of dealing with the problem worked. For instance, when they came across a lion, our ancestors either ran away, avoided the lion's territory, or attacked it (with weapons and as a group). Escaping, avoiding, and aggressing are all rewarded ways of dealing with challenges.

In modern times, we've also invented fantastic things to control challenging situations in our external environment. Insulated homes let us escape the heat in the summer and cold in the winter. We avoid hurting our feet by wearing shoes. People sometimes smack the side of a faulty machine to "fix" loose connections. These are all ways we try to control the experiences we're faced with, and oftentimes they lead to successful outcomes.

It's logical that since we are well-rewarded for controlling our external environment, we would also try to control our internal environment. However, those same methods of control that served us so well in dealing with predators, bad weather, rough ground, and broken machines, are not so helpful when it comes to addressing internal-world issues. One way an otherwise physically harmless situation might be aversive is when you feel emotions you would prefer not to experience—like sadness, anger, fear, anxiety, dread, or even boredom. We can escape and avoid situations that make us uncomfortable, and sometimes that's fine and healthy. But escaping, avoiding, and lashing out at our emotions isn't a worthwhile long-term strategy for facing life in a values-based manner. For example, avoiding studying a topic you find demanding and boring isn't going to help you pass a test, even though avoiding will—in the short term—help you to control the unpleasant experience of frustration and boredom. Avoiding this experience comes with a cost, because you'll either eventually find yourself cramming for the exam with the same boring and incomprehensible material, or failing the test because you could not deal with the feelings. Either of these consequences will once again bring up other thoughts and feelings. When aversive situations are inside our own bodies, and we try to avoid them, we're trapped. You really can't escape or avoid your own feelings no matter how hard you try. To illustrate this problem, let's meet Cal.

● *Cal's Story*

Cal is struggling. After experiencing a grueling divorce and professional burnout, they quit their job as an art teacher in middle-school to return to a career in the visual arts. They dreamed of living as a creative artist when they were younger, but that was sidelined by the demands of working and raising kids, as well as by the emotional drain of a toxic marriage. Cal was privileged to have inherited a house and enough money to live on for a while, so they allotted a year to create a fresh start for themself and for their two elementary school-aged children.

However, three months in, Cal isn't even entering their studio most mornings, and instead fills their days with yoga classes and making cute organic lunches for the kids. Sometimes they just spend the afternoon with a bottle of wine and cooking an elaborate dinner, even though they know the kids would be happy with spaghetti. They've been excusing these digressions from their career goals by thinking they need time to focus on their fitness and that specialized nutrition is crucial for the children. Deep-down Cal knows that's not why they aren't making art. When Cal did the Life Atlas exercise, they identified four core valued domains: creating art, parenting, relationships, and physical/emotional well-being. But they were "Not at All" feeling Global Harmony, and they were as far "Lost" as they could be for the creating art domain. After identifying art-related values of "creativity," "sustainability," "self-expression," "engaging with the community," and "lifelong learning/improvement," Cal had set goals to spend at least four hours a day, five days a week in the studio. However, at this point they barely go into the studio for an hour, and mostly spend time reorganizing their materials. Now when they even look at the door to the studio, they feel dread about their future and fear of career failure. Cal starts to ruminate: How could I have been so irresponsible as to quit my job? My ex was probably right…I am selfish, frivolous, and certain to fail! I'm a horrible parent! *No matter how much Cal tries to make the dread and fear go away, the feelings remain and get bigger and stronger. The more they avoid these feelings by staying away from the studio, the worse it gets! No art and no money are being made, which exacerbates the dread, fear, and guilt, and it seems to be a downward spiral.*

Did reading about Cal's struggles touch a nerve for you? Take a moment now and think about a domain on your Life Atlas where you feel lost or stuck. Are there actions on your MAP you're having difficulty doing because they bring up emotions you'd prefer not to experience? What emotions potentially block your forward movement on your valued actions?

_____

_____

_____

_____

_____

Name Your Feelings

Before looking at how you can learn to "accept" the difficult feelings that arise in difficult circumstances, there's a critical first step. To get more flexible at responding to such situations, you need to become aware of and skilled at observing feelings, sensations, urges, and emotions along with the context in which they take place. You began to practice this in the last chapter with the "Contact the Present Emotion" exercise.

Most of us aren't very good at precisely identifying our feelings and naming them for what they are. This is partly because we each experience emotions in our own unique way, and it's hard to learn how to name emotions that only you sense. We're stuck with learning how to name our feelings based on what others (like our caregivers in early childhood) tell us we might be feeling given particular circumstances. If a child drops their ice cream cone and starts crying, their caregiver might say how "sad" they must be, and if another child takes their toy and they start crying, their caregiver might talk about how "mad" that must make them feel. Sometimes these labels are accurate, but sometimes they're not. And sometimes we're not given labels for our emotions at all; we're left to figure out for ourselves what we're feeling and what we ought to do about it. Either way, learning to tune in to our circumstances and our internal world in more subtle ways than how we've been taught is challenging. Most of us need to practice this regularly throughout our lives.

To improve your ability to name your emotions, start to notice the subtleties in the circumstances that show up in a given situation. Researchers in the UCLA Social Cognitive Neuroscience Lab suggest that observing and naming emotions has a powerful impact all on its own. The brain research implies that when the area related to our executive functions (i.e., thinking, remembering, organizing, self-control) is active, the area related to feeling emotional responses has reduced likelihood of activity. Put simply (and in a way neurologists might think is oversimplification), when your brain takes up energy to name what you feel, there is diminished energy in the part of the brain related to actually feeling it. Naming your feelings helps you regulate them, and the less energy they are given, the easier it is to observe them for what they are: sensations and emotions that you can choose to respond to in a flexible manner.

One way to get better at identifying what's going on inside your body is to begin by identifying in more detail what's going on outside your body and paying attention to the information those details give you. It might seem a bit silly at first, but let's take the example of clouds, which are often available for us to pay attention to, but we usually don't. Clouds come in many different forms, each of which has a specific name: nimbus, cumulus, cumulonimbus, stratus, and so on. Can you spend a few minutes every day this week looking at the clouds and noticing the details that help you to classify them? What does the shape of the cloud tell you about current and likely future weather patterns? Does that give you useful information for your day, like taking an umbrella with you? When you get better at observing clouds, you can more successfully predict what might be coming next and prepare yourself to aptly handle it.

Ultimately, identifying your own emotions, like identifying cloud formations, takes practice. Start now by closing your eyes and scanning your body beginning with your toes and moving up to your head. How does each part feel right now? Tense? Relaxed? Heavy? Light? Make note of this here before you move on.

_____

_____

_____

Now, think for a moment about a time when you felt a strong emotion. Can you identify what sensations you felt in your body?

_____

_____

_____

_____

When you were feeling this strong emotion, what thoughts were you having? Were you invalidating your emotions by thinking you shouldn't be feeling this way?

_____

_____

_____

_____

What behaviors followed this experience? Did the feeling assist you in flexible action, or did you find yourself blocked from valued behavior?

_____

_____

_____

_____

Typically, it's challenging to articulate and pinpoint our emotional responses—this skill takes practice. For now, see what you can accomplish when you imagine yourself in that situation—it can be a situation that you felt great about or a situation that was painful. Think about what you felt in your body, how you spoke to yourself, and if that increased or decreased values-based behavior.

Exercise: Identifying Feelings

Practice identifying your physical feelings, thoughts, and emotions at many different points throughout the day. Set four random alarms on your smartphone each day over the next few days. Whenever the alarm goes off, spend the next minute noting the situation you find yourself in, scanning how your body feels, identifying the thoughts arising, and labeling the emotion without judgment. Use the following table for this exercise.

Time	Situation	Physical Feeling	Thoughts	Emotion Label

If you struggle with labeling how you feel, refer to the Emotion Wheel that follows. When starting from the inner circle, you might be able to more aptly discriminate the broader, fundamental feeling, and then you can move to the outer circle in that wedge to more finely describe how you feel. Please note that there are many versions of this type of wheel—there's no one definitive way to categorize every emotion, so if you find yourself using other terms in other ways, that is perfectly fine. Here, too, we support being flexible.

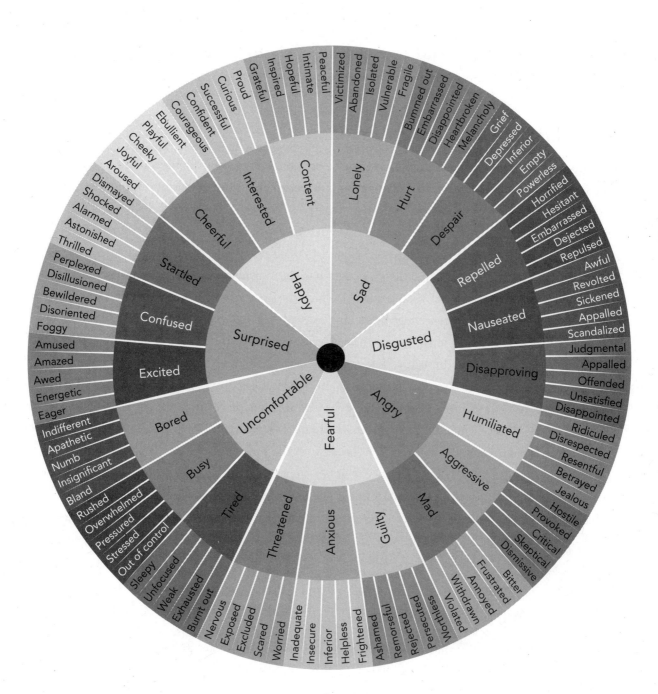

You can continue to do this activity using the worksheet available for download at http://www. newharbinger.com/50713. Do this for as long as you find it helpful in assessing your emotions. As you continue working with this skill of identifying your feelings precisely, understand that it's also important to be able to identify when you're feeling relaxed as well as tense. Becoming fluent at identifying all your emotions can assist with the skill of acceptance.

The Challenge of Negative Emotions

As you completed the activity of describing your emotions, you probably found yourself evaluating the feelings you had, despite our instructions to not be judgmental! In our culture, feelings like fear, sadness, and anger have been labeled "negative" emotions. We talk about these feelings as being difficult, or bad, or heavy—they are hard to bear. As we discussed in chapter 2, in the three-step process of language, *describing* and *evaluating* are followed by *problem-solving*. We can describe a feeling (sadness), evaluate it (negative), and then we might have been conditioned to solve the problem of a negative emotion. We try to "fix" these kinds of feelings, the same way we would want to fix a broken machine. You might "fix" your feelings by seeking therapy, turning to aerobic exercises, or reciting positive affirmations. Or you might escape through alcohol, avoid through overexercising, or aggress with the negative emotion through self-destructive acts. In addition, your "fixing" could simply involve outright avoidance—you could simply choose not to do the things that bring up those negative emotions. Because those types of experiential avoidance seem successful—for a little while—you just might keep doing them, even though they're actually exacerbating the problem in the long run. Cal's methods of avoiding are quite insidious because on the surface, they seem healthy and values-directed. Doing yoga and cooking for their children appears justifiable, but they're really used to avoid facing fear. And the more time Cal spends with yoga and cooking, the less art is being created, which in turn increases the fear, which calls for soothing by going to the yoga studio or trying a new recipe, and so on. Significant problems occur when "the solution" is actually the problem! This is where accepting the "negative" emotions is crucial for moving forward on your chosen path.

Do Negative Emotions Exist?

As we examine the fact that avoiding "negative" emotions can become problematic, contemplate this question: Are there truly *negative* emotions? Can you consider that the ways you *feel* are not "negative," but *saying* they are "negative" makes the experience problematic? Perhaps society *conditions* us to label feelings as "negative," and then we're influenced to avoid or get rid of those emotions because they are "negative." And such efforts typically don't work well. In fact, by avoiding them, the emotions persevere or become more intense because we're not facing them.

Clearly, there are feelings associated with traumatic, painful external-world events. But the question is, are the emotions the negative part of the experience, or is it the external events that provoked the emotions? Consider this: you've been taught by society to *describe* how you feel (anxious, sad, etc.), and then taught to *evaluate* these feelings as "negative" by society's norms. We're not criticizing you for thinking this way! Top-notch psychology journals, best-selling books, and even writings by the Dalai Lama sometimes call some of the ways we feel "negative" emotions. But what if that terminology perpetuates a problematic viewpoint about these ancient internal experiences by calling them "negative"?

These feelings have been experienced by humans for eons, and we inherit the ability to feel emotions because they increase the odds we'll survive. Our feelings of fear prepare us to deal with dangerous threats, and feelings of sadness after losing something important help us slow down and recover from the loss. Tears from crying can only be seen by someone close, and the tears work as a signal showing need for social support after dealing with the loss. Our primary emotions have been selected for their survival function. These aren't negative emotions to be avoided, but *natural emotions* to be accepted.

What if you could view the way you feel as a natural emotion, instead of something to get rid of? Review your history and see how often you've been told not to feel the way that you naturally feel. We often hear phrases like these:

- "There, there… don't be sad!"

- "Don't get mad at me!"

- "Stop worrying so much!"

- "Can't you just be happy about this?"

Let's say someone is feeling scared, and a person who is trying to "fix" that negative emotion shouts, "Calm down!" Does that ever work? No. Instead it typically exacerbates the feeling!

Rather than trying to control them, which isn't possible, acceptance is an effective and helpful approach for dealing with these feelings. Even with more complex, intense behavioral health issues, such as anxiety and depression, being willing to experience natural emotions for what they are—without trying to get rid of them—is the effective way to deal with the distress. Embracing these natural emotions without needlessly pushing them away supports psychological flexibility, mental health, and mindful action.

A Closer Look at Reacting to Emotions

What emotion do you struggle with the most? Is it anger, anxiety, sadness, something else, or is it a painful combination of all those? Dare yourself to bring that feeling up now. Use your imagination to remember situations or people that really intensified these feelings. Using that misnomer for the last time, what "negative" emotions did you feel?

_____

_____

_____

_____

Take a moment to sit with your emotion related to these memories or evaluations.

Now, in what ways have you tried to control, "fix," or avoid these feelings?

_____

_____

_____

_____

In what ways have those efforts worked for you?

_____

_____

_____

_____

What have those efforts cost you? How have they made things more problematic?

_____

_____

_____

_____

Can you see these feelings as a natural part of your human condition? That doesn't mean they were comfortable, or that you deserved such pain. Given the complexity of the world, these feelings might not make sense to you. But can you see that feeling this way naturally arises as part of being human? Knowing that feelings are part of being human, how does that change your memory? Does that make your memory of the experience softer in some way—easier to understand and to handle?

_____

_____

_____

_____

It may take some practice to view your emotions in this way, but thinking of emotions as "natural" instead of "negative" can support accepting them, and can also change how you view the situation in which the feelings arose.

Accepting: Being Willing to Have Natural Emotions

You've probably gotten the point that trying to escape, avoid, or otherwise control your feelings is simply unworkable, unhelpful, and leads to psychological inflexibility. Being unwilling to feel what you feel blocks you from completing items on your to-do list or achieving valued goals you've elaborated on your MAP, and it keeps you further away from living a valued life. Accepting is the opposite approach, and the MAP reminds you to be willing to face your feelings when you'd rather not. Accepting is about allowing what arises, rather than resisting it, so that you'll be able to focus on what you value doing in ways you won't be able to if you keep fighting or avoiding what you call "negative" emotions. And valuing means that you care deeply enough about the directions you're going that you're willing to accept the feelings and go through whatever difficulty or pain might be necessary to keep moving forward on your path. Accepting is wearing the horrible sweater your grandmother made for you, even though it's ugly because it reminds you of her. Accepting is receiving both sides of the values coin, the joy *and* the pain that arise as we pursue our purpose, as a gift. Accepting means that you not only tolerate adversity, but that you also willingly walk into it—like walking onto your stage and embracing your feelings that reveal to you just how much you care.

If you're struggling with this—and wondering, *How can I accept being sad* (or angry, or any other feeling)?—another way to think about acceptance is as *willingness*. Can you be *willing* to feel pain rather than try to control it, in order to do the things that are important to you? Feel free to use the term "willingness" instead if it fits better for you.

Take a few moments to see if this idea really resonates with you. What we're offering here is a culturally unusual approach to relating to your feelings. We live in a society where we get rewarded for getting rid of "negative" things. But what if you can change your perspective on these feelings in your internal world? We're truly advocating for an alternate approach: to see them as a gift—not in a frivolous or sappy "every rose has its thorn" way, but with wisdom and maturity. Realize you feel these ancient emotions because they're a good source of information about how we're interacting with the world and what's motivating us to act—just like the cloud patterns give us information to help us plan for the weather. They're a signal that you're meaningfully connecting to your path. When you feel certain ways, you can actually use those feelings to fuel values-based actions. The catch is to harness this emotional motivation and use it to act toward your values.

● *Cal's Story*

Once Cal began to identify their emotions and see more clearly how they were sidestepping the studio to avoid the fear and dread that seemed to accompany it, they pondered what these feelings were telling them. As an artist, they knew all emotions could be drivers for creativity—why had they not thought to use their emotions in their art instead of pushing them to the side? Wrapped up in the emotions were thoughts and worries for the future of their family, and Cal also saw that part of the tangled web of feelings included impatience—a feeling of urgency to do something big and important with their time, and a fear that they wouldn't. The evidence was in front of them every day that they weren't doing anything particularly remarkable. Cal sat with these feelings for a long time before seeing that, in fact, their work needed to slow down, not speed up—but first it needed to actually start. If they could start, it didn't matter how long it took—the art would unfold at the speed it demanded. They determined to willingly work with their emotions in their art—painting the fear, sculpting the guilt, sketching the impatience—and see where that could take them.

Exploring Emotions

Return now to your MAP and any actions you haven't been doing, as well as the domains on your Life Atlas where you feel lost or stuck. Note the natural feelings you identified at the beginning of this chapter as arising in that context. You've already identified ways in which you may have avoided these feelings. Can you think now of what more they might be telling you about the situation? Are there links to your values underneath these emotions that might give you important information about the next step on your path? Make some notes about this here, as well as noting a few key words in the Accepting section of your MAP about what you might need to make space for.

_____

_____

_____

_____

Understanding the Edges of Acceptance

Before we go on, we want to emphasize that acceptance is not the same as hopeless resignation or simply tolerating an arduous situation. Giving up, being beaten down by circumstances, and simply ceasing to care are not indications of acceptance. There are also situations in which acceptance is not the appropriate aim. For instance, if you're locked in an abusive relationship or toxic workplace, "accepting your fate" is not helpful or appropriate, and this is *not* what we mean by acceptance. If there are actions you can take to improve your situation, whether that means following doctor's orders if you've been diagnosed with an illness, seeking professional therapy if you have signs of depression or are experiencing thoughts of self-harm, or exploring your options for leaving a harmful situation, you're encouraged to engage in self-care. Acceptance will still be helpful because it'll allow you to deal with the difficult thoughts and feelings arising as you take the necessary actions. In fact, in such circumstances, acceptance is vital to surmounting the difficulties that taking such actions present.

If you're in an urgent situation like this, jot down the directions for action the previous discussion might have inspired. Consider what's currently keeping you in the sticky situation or causing you to avoid the actions you could take, and also consider that professional help is likely necessary to support your actions. In the end, keep this in mind: escaping, avoiding, and lashing out to try to control your emotions and your world will ultimately narrow your possibilities. Your capacity for accepting opens up new possibilities and encourages doing what you care about.

Be Kind to Yourself

Now that you're learning to identify your emotions more precisely and to describe them as occurring within a particular context, we hope you're also beginning to recognize how normal it is to feel pain as well as joy. Feelings are part of our common humanity—not an indication that we're broken and need fixing. However, at times, most of us judge ourselves and even beat ourselves up for having emotions. Have you ever berated yourself for being sad for "too long" about a breakup, or not getting a job you wanted, or anything else? Would you have judged a close friend in the same way, or would you have been more compassionate? When you read Cal's thoughts about being selfish and a horrible parent, did you want to provide comfort and kindness?

When you identify your values, are any of them related to how you positively and socially interact with others? If so, what would it be like to consider your interactions with *yourself* in terms of these same values? If you aim to be kind, fair, and thoughtful to other people, can you do the same for yourself? If we're going to accept our hard feelings and willingly engage in the activities that bring up hard feelings, then it helps to take it easy on ourselves for having those feelings. We can all use a little help being *self*-compassionate and recognizing that our emotions, sensations, urges, and other feelings are simply part of being human.

EXERCISE: Being a Kind Coach

For this exercise, you'll need two pieces of paper to write two letters to yourself. Write "Dear [your name]" at the top of each page. The first letter will be from your "Inner Critic" and the second from a "Kind Coach."[1]

Spend a few moments thinking about a recent situation that brought up a lot of challenging natural emotions, including negative evaluations of yourself and/or your performance. This might

---

1   This exercise is adapted from Fiebig, Gould, Ming, and Watson (2021) *Acting on a Value of Self-Care*. Workshop for Constellations Community of Practice. Used with permission.

come from situations you've been thinking about related to those actions that you aren't doing on your MAP, or it could be another recent event that comes to mind. Consider the elements that were hard for you. When you're ready, set a timer for five minutes and write all the things your Inner Critic might say about that experience and who you are as a person.

When you're done, read what you wrote and reflect on your experience. What did you notice? Did the criticisms come quickly? Was the voice of your Inner Critic familiar? Did you notice yourself censoring or curating what you wrote? Did anything surprise you? What do you feel when reading what you wrote?

The second letter you write will be from a Kind Coach. Spend a few moments imagining the following: Someone you love is experiencing a similar difficult situation. Picture them truly struggling. Imagine they write to you and ask for support and advice. What might you say? What might you do to offer support? Think about this for a few more moments. What might you want to hear when you are suffering? Set your timer for five minutes and begin.

When you're done, shift into the perspective of the person you were writing to—read what you wrote and reflect on your experience. What did you notice? How did it feel to be spoken to from a Kind Coach perspective? Was it challenging in any way? Was the voice of your Kind Coach familiar? Did you notice yourself censoring or curating what you wrote? Did anything surprise you? When looking at your letter, what do you feel?

Make Friends with What Pains You

The language you use about your feelings is central to your experience of them. Your language can create suffering by reminding you of past aversive circumstances or worrying about intimidating future events. But our language can also alleviate suffering, and even create joy in response to that same event. In chapter 4, you leveraged your values to help motivate you to do actions you were avoiding. We can also connect our values to hard feelings themselves. When we can see these feelings as indicators of us doing something arduous and important, they not only become bearable, but also welcomed.

Return again to your MAP, to the Doing section and to the actions that you have not been doing as well as the natural feelings you identified as arising in that context. Return to the values that the actions and feelings are connected to. What are the ways in which you can use these feelings as reminders of how you're doing something meaningful, perhaps even being grateful for that reminder from your mind?

_____

_____

_____

_____

● *Cal's Story*

As Cal struggles with their major life changes, they are also becoming wiser and more psychologically flexible. When fear of not being a good artist arises, they notice what their mind is saying, and rather than struggling with the feelings, they attend to the values linked to the pain they feel—remembering that they hurt because they care about their art. They might say, "I can feel my heart racing, so I know I'm afraid that I won't live up to my own expectations. I fear my art will not be good enough for me to make a living. Thank you, mind, for reminding me of how important it is for me to commit to my art as a gift of creative expression to myself and to the world, and how brave I am for doing something so hard. By persisting in this challenge, I'm giving a good example to my children to commit to the hard work of staying true to their values in life." In taking this approach, Cal demonstrates willingness to harness natural emotions in the service of doing what they care about, even though they were taught to label those feelings as "negative."

Now that Cal has had practice sitting with and identifying their feelings and is learning to embrace them as part of doing a challenging and deeply meaningful activity, they are ready to continue their commitment to their goals. They made a sign for the door of their studio: "You have to make lots of bad art to make good art." They're committed to putting the time in to creating art, feeling the exertion, letting emotions arise without trying to control them, and trusting their skills and the process. Every day they've set both a time-in-studio goal and a production goal—producing without judgment of quality, simply giving themself the space to practice and find their way. They've added these daily goals to their MAP in the Doing section. They've also added a reflection task—being curious about how the experience is every day and practicing compassion for themself in the same way they would treat their children. They created a MAP phrase for themself: "I am here now, accepting and harnessing my feelings of fear and guilt, noticing my thoughts about being frivolous and untalented, while creating the art I find meaningful."

How about you? Take the time now to clarify, add to, commit to your goals, then identify how you can make space for natural emotions arising as you take further steps on your path.

_____

_____

_____

_____

Moving Forward

This chapter focused on acceptance and aimed to help you recognize that it's not viable to try to control your feelings. It is, however, possible—and even valuable—to willingly engage in actions that bring up tough feelings, to learn to embrace them as part of the process, and to harness them to do what you care about. Acceptance also helps promote the kinds of mindfulness you began practicing in the last chapter, leading to more effective mindful action. You learned to become more aware of your feelings (including the thoughts going along with them), learning to name them and attending to the contexts in which they occur. You also learned to connect your feelings to your values and to recognize that your feelings give you useful information about what's important to you. We presented a number of different practices that help to increase your willingness to experience difficult feelings while committing to the actions that help you achieve your goals. These practices work to keep your feelings from presenting obstacles to mindful action.

With these tools, you gain more skills for traveling the path with psychological flexibility! We hope you're finding your way using your MAP to guide you in spotting and working with the obstacles that arise as you pursue your valued directions. In the next chapter, we'll introduce more tools for unhooking from the obstacles your mind puts in your way—your own thoughts.

CHAPTER 8

Noticing

By this point in the workbook, you've established values-based goals and begun using the MAP to assist you in doing what you care about. You've also learned to maintain contact with the here and now and to accept your emotions as you engage in your chosen actions. Now we'll turn your attention to another way you inadvertently take detours or stop moving forward on your journey: getting stuck in your own thoughts. While completing your Life Atlas and practicing mindful action exercises in previous chapters, you may have experienced thoughts that distracted you from valued behavior. You might find yourself hooked by what you're saying to yourself and simply unable to focus on moving forward. The MAP was created to help you with this obstacle too.

A Piece of the MAP: Noticing

	Observe thoughts that arise while moving forward with valued actions. Let those thoughts go if they are not helpful. Treat distracting thoughts as disconnected from action while choosing to act in a meaningful manner.	

The MAP is a checklist for a psychologically flexible journey. It advises travelers to prepare to detach from thoughts that arise while moving forward with valued actions and to let those thoughts go if they aren't helpful. In addition, the MAP suggests treating distracting thoughts as disconnected from action while choosing to act in a meaningful manner.

"Let those thoughts go" is easier said than done! But learning mindfulness exercises to help you contact the here and now, and releasing the emotional control agenda with acceptance practices are also instances of learning to "let go." You can develop a more functional relationship with your language so that thoughts don't sway you from your chosen path. In acceptance and commitment therapy, this skill is called "defusion," and we call it Noticing on the MAP.

This skill encourages you to not take your thoughts literally but rather to simply observe what you're thinking. You notice your thoughts, but you don't allow those thoughts to have a significant or problematic influence on your actions. Noticing is when you look *at* your thoughts rather than *from* your thoughts. In other words, you're observing the mind's "stuff"—the languaging—while *not* letting that stuff have an impact on how you see the world and how you behave in it. Noticing is an essential wayfinding skill: it allows you to take a bird's-eye view of your environment, to identify where you're being led astray, and to see the path forward in the direction of your values.

Private languaging—self-talk—can be critically important when you're dealing with a challenging task. The power of language is a gift that helps you accomplish your aim. For example, you might be hiking on a path, look down at your feet, and realize you have a problem. Your languaging kicks in: "My shoe is untied" (describe). "That's dangerous because I'm hiking" (evaluate). "I'll tie my shoe in a double-knot this time to fix it and prevent it from happening again" (problem-solve). This describing, evaluating, and problem-solving language is rewarded by accomplishing tasks and removing problems that trip you up on your journey. Clearly, this oversimplifies how minds work, but the point is that your language helps you influence the world around you, and it's reinforced well by desired consequences. This languaging skill surfaces frequently because it's so helpful, and you inadvertently use it all the time. This is how the gift becomes a curse.

The problem arises when you get so used to using language that you can't stop, even when it's unhelpful. While you're doing what you care about, language sometimes pops up in counterproductive ways. Let's take a look at that kind of problematic influence as we meet Ali.

◆ Ali's Story

Ali's promotion from being a line operator in a paper mill to the dayshift safety manager was, just like language, a gift and a curse. Ali's authentic occupational values of "improving the quality of life for people," "safety," and "being a good provider" were definitely being served with this new position, and the salary increase was quite welcome. But the job was a taxing middle-management position, and her new task at work was reducing incidents and injuries for 300 millworkers. She found this very stressful.

Ultimately, Ali wanted to make an impact and maintain her work relationships with everyone she knew in the mill, but her coworkers did not embrace her role change, so they occasionally disregarded her management attempts. Sometimes midshift, Ali would think, I suck at this job. It's pointless trying to do good things around here. It's probably better if I don't bother! *Other thoughts cropped up throughout the day about her lack of skill as a manager, and these thoughts caused her to withdraw from doing positive tasks she'd planned to reduce injuries at the worksite.*

Does Ali's story resonate with you? Are there areas of your Life Atlas or specific actions on your MAP where language sends you into an unproductive spiral? Can you see how sometimes you're stuck on your path because you're tangled up in thoughts about the challenging situation and your own insecurities and judgments? When this does occur, what do you say to yourself? Make notes about your problematic thinking here.

_____

_____

_____

_____

_____

_____

_____

As you consider how your own thoughts might be tripping you up, be gentle with yourself—in other contexts you've reaped the benefits of your mind's wonderful ability to describe, evaluate, and problem-solve. As we mentioned earlier, humans have evolved to communicate in order to get more good and less bad in life. The problem is that language is so helpful that we keep languaging even when it isn't helpful! As the saying goes, when all you have is a hammer, everything looks like a nail. For instance, in chapter 7 when you learned about accepting your emotions, you also learned that you sometimes act in unhelpful ways to escape, avoid, or get rid of the feelings. Your mind describes what you feel and evaluates it as "negative," and then problem-solves to get rid of the "negative" stuff. Unfortunately, those attempts backfire and aren't much of a solution. The languaging that can be so beneficial for solving problems can also go awry. Under certain circumstances, our language creates rigidity rather than flexibility. Defusion, or noticing, helps loosen up those rigid patterns.

Defusion's Other Side: Cognitive Fusion

To understand how to unhook from the kinds of thoughts that trap you and Ali, we have to understand fusion. In a broad sense, fusion is defined as joining two or more things together forming a single entity. On a construction site, a welder might use a torch to fuse two pieces of metal together to make it one entity. In ACT, fusion metaphorically implies that two things will form a single entity: your behavior and your thoughts! *Cognitive fusion* is when actions get strongly and rigidly influenced by thoughts. People do this all the time. Imagine when a basketball player goes for a free throw, and says to herself, *I'll never make this shot.* Fusion to this negative self-talk impedes good form and concentration, and she misses the basket. In football, an opposing coach will call a time-out right before the other team's kicker goes for a field goal. The coach is diabolically trying to "get the kicker up in his head" before attempting the three-pointer. Sports aficionados call this "icing the kicker" because the time-out has the potential to freeze up the athlete's performance by sending a chill to their confidence. This time-out is intended to aggravate and irritate the player (which is a good opportunity for *accepting* feelings on the kicker's part) and can also cause fusion to self-doubt and second guessing, distracting the kicker from the necessary focus on performance (which is a good opportunity for *noticing* thoughts). Fusion to negative self-talk drags down performance. This is why there's often trash talk in competition: in addition to competitors trying to physically thwart the other team's performance, they often try to mentally impede their performance with language too. But if athletes could dispassionately notice when language is present (whether it's their own or the opponent's) and relate to it objectively as if it were just a noisy bunch of sounds, then such language wouldn't have to influence their actions.

Whether you're an athlete or not, you probably do some trash talking to yourself at times. You don't need someone else saying denigrating things to you because you do a perfectly fine job all on your own! More specifically, people have already said denigrating things to you, maybe even a long time ago, and you "internalized" it. Because of the human condition, and how our brain is wired, we fuse to that kind of language, and it can pop up again at unfortunate times.

Sizing Up Your Own Worst Enemy

How are you reacting to this discussion of problematic thoughts? You might resonate with it because this is an obvious part of the human condition. We all have memories of mistakes we've made because we were "psyched out" by our own self-talk. You're about to do an exercise about these crummy memories, which has the potential to lead to a dejected mood state. Make sure you have the time and space to do this exercise, and to process it afterward.

EXERCISE: The "Could Not" and the "Must"

In this exercise, you'll review times in your life when your thoughts impeded you from doing what you care about. We encourage you to choose memories from valued parts of your history, and from important sections of your Life Atlas. Recall times in your life when your thoughts stopped you from moving forward on desired aims.

You'll be exploring two areas of problematic language: when you told yourself (1) you *could not* do something and (2) you *must* do something, and how it turned into a problem for following through on valued action. (To reiterate, make sure this is about thoughts leading to a resulting problem. Sometimes it's beneficial to ward off problems with "musts" and "could nots," but that's not what we're asking here.) Think of when you *could not* do something—such as asking your boss for a raise, applying for a school, or getting out of bed while depressed—because of self-doubt. Recall a situation when you told yourself you *could not* do things successfully, what problem came up, and what you were cognitively fused to that influenced that problem. In other words, you looked at the world from these thoughts in a literal way and the language problematically influenced your valued actions and psychological flexibility. Write down those thoughts and the context where they occurred. Take your time with this and see if it can relate to important areas of your Life Atlas.

The "Could Not..."

The situation when I told myself I *could not* do something was _____

and it led me to the problem of _____

because I was specifically thinking _____.

Next, bring up another example of problematic language, and focus on a time you told yourself you *must* do something, but it ended up being a bad outcome. Examples include rigidly telling yourself you must deliver a cruel insult to a partner or you must impulsively allow yourself to break your nutrition plan and eat that chocolate cupcake, or rationalizing that you must have a cocktail even though you've been sober for twenty-nine days and you're about to get your one-month chip from your AA sponsor. Pick something where you told yourself you *must* do an action, became fused to the thoughts, looked at the world from these thoughts in a literal way, and then they problematically influenced your valued actions. Take your time with this one, too, and see if it can relate to important areas of your Life Atlas.

The "Must…"

The situation when I told myself I *must* do something was _____

and it led me to the problem of _____

because I was specifically thinking _____.

_____

Now look at what you wrote on the final, fused content line for "The 'Could Not' and the 'Must'" exercise. Review what you said to yourself that blocked movement toward your goals or thwarted you from a valued direction. If those words even partly altered forward motion on your life's journey, that's fusion! Two things became one: your preventing thoughts melded with prevented actions. Your mental inhibitions led to inhibited behavior. This is reminiscent of Henry Ford's quip, "Whether you think you can, or you think you can't—you're right!" Ford isn't 100 percent correct with this oft-used phrase, but there is a bit of wisdom to consider. If you're fused to thoughts, then Henry's viewpoint is correct. Choose to make him incorrect and yourself defused!

"Could nots" and "musts" aren't the only ways we damage our own progress. You can also botch things up by insulting yourself ("I'm a nogoodnik"), believing unhelpful rules ("It's better if I don't assert myself in my relationship"), and endorsing things that are factually incorrect ("The world is an awful place"). For example, Ali impeded her leadership actions with these three types of problematic thoughts when she said to herself, *I suck at this job. It's pointless trying to do good things around here. It's probably better if I don't bother!* When fusion takes over, and she thinks she can't, she's right, just as Ford asserted! Keep in mind something very important about Ali's role: she's a safety manager in charge of reducing injuries for 300 people. How she relates to her thoughts contributes to how the mill is managed, and if it's mismanaged, it could have life-and-death consequences. If she's fused to her thinking, she not only misses out on valued behavior, but other people might too! This is one reason why ACTraining and the Mindful Action Plan belong in the workplace.

Because of the myriad ways human beings generate language, there are many ways your thoughts can lead you astray or impede progress on your path. Fusion has an undue, unwelcome effect on the way you live your life, and defusion, or noticing, helps you untangle from the unhelpfulness of language. Keep this in mind though: it's not so much what *form* your thoughts take, but what matters is the *function* of your thinking. To say it another way, you can have lots of unconstructive, irrational, and distorted thoughts throughout the day—and you probably do throughout your life—but you don't have to follow through on them! It's not *what* you think, but *how you relate to* what you're thinking! Noticing problematic thoughts, instead of getting hooked by them, makes room for mindful action.

Changing How We Look at Language

You're currently letting shapes and symbols on this page hold your attention. Language is influencing your behavior. Now take the perspective that these symbols and shapes don't have to have any impact. They are, after all, simply words. You were conditioned to think in a way that these words have meaningful impact on yourself and your actions, but they don't have to have influence on you. Fow, zumptan nildy harmonshoo chiggy harssan–tolik dra waiz–vandagarn quall umsa lageewan. Reading those words was probably a weird experience because they are functionally meaningless, but they are formally readable. They seem a lot like the typical language you use daily, but that sentence is just a bunch of made-up words.

Here's the thing: *all language is just a bunch of made-up words!* You were taught to let these squiggles and lines influence your emotions and actions, but they don't actually *have to* cause you to feel or act a certain way. In the same way, you have the ability to just notice that strange sentence. It was present, but it didn't actually instruct you to feel or do anything specifically, and therefore, you just let it go by. You weren't attached to those words in any particular way. They didn't move you. Here's the thing about defusion and Noticing: you don't have to be attached or moved by any words if you choose not to be!

Go back to "The 'Could Not' and the 'Must'" exercise, and look for a phrase that influenced an unhelpful outcome in your life. Take another look at what you wrote, and then view it in a different manner. See what you wrote as ink marks on paper. Observe those words that obstructed action as just squiggles and lines. This is a step to defusing from the power of this language. Simply notice that you wrote words related to what you once thought. These squiggles and lines aren't "truths" or dogma or magic spells. These words don't have to have an impact on you.

Now rewrite those words. Rewrite the symbols and shapes of that problematic fused content again a few times, and each time vary your handwriting.

Use your nondominant hand: _____

Print it: _____

Write it in cursive: _____

Hold the pen like a three-year-old: _____

Attempt calligraphy: _____

Scrawl it like a doctor's handwriting: _____

Write with hieroglyphics (*just pretend!*): _____

Draw the letters like it is a signature: _____

Jot it down backward: _____

Observe the effects of repeating those words. Sometimes writing words over and over reduces the impact and meaning of the language. If you catch even a glimpse of how these words lose a bit of power, that tells you something very important: Words do not *have to* control you. They don't *have to* cause action. Your thoughts do not make you do things. They certainly have influenced you, but you can learn to relate to them differently. Robots might be compelled by computer programming, but humans aren't forced to act according to their thoughts.

When you looked at the world *from* those thoughts, they influenced problematic actions or non-action. This time look *at* those thoughts you wrote. Look at each iteration from a distance. They aren't happening "between your ears and behind your eyes" as thoughts. You can detach from this language. Gaze at what you wrote and attempt to see the arbitrariness of these shapes and symbols. Back when you were thinking these thoughts, they were so impactful and influenced your actions in a problematic way. Now they're just ink on paper, and the ink cannot influence your actions. Your private experiences of language can be treated the same way!

Now, remaining aware that these were thoughts, try just *privately thinking* the words in different ways. Using that problematic content, do this "in your head," so to speak:

Sing it like an opera singer.

Say it in a robot voice.

Whisper it (*yes, in your head!*).

Scream it (*seriously, you can do this with your thoughts*).

Sing it like a heavy metal vocalist.

Say it like it would sound spoken underwater.

You might have just realized that you can have some influence on reducing the power of your thoughts. Saying this stuff in different ways shows that language isn't completely in control of *you*! You had these thoughts in the past, and if they return, treat them as disconnected from your overt behavior. In many ways, this is what the traditional mindfulness exercises are typically trying to teach!

Predicting Fused Content

Now that we've looked at some old, fused content that prevented valued action in the past, let's see if we can predict some problems in the future. Take a look at the actions you planned in the Doing section of your MAP. Now explore the potential obstacles your mind will conjure up. Examine if your mind is churning out language in the same way Ali's mind did, like *It's probably better if I don't bother!* If you have fused thoughts, they're likely to be more specific to your own journey. We can only guess, but perhaps you're thinking things such as *I really don't deserve this to happen for me, I ain't got the smarts to accomplish this,* or *Nobody gives a dang if I do this, so why should I?* Just because you have such thoughts doesn't mean they're true or that they have to have an impact on you!

What thoughts are arising around your goals and values? If your thoughts are all about excitement and positivity, good for you! But be careful with those thoughts too. Sometimes language can lead to overconfidence and so much hype that we don't prepare enough for the journey, and outcomes don't hit the mark. The mind isn't necessarily your enemy, but it isn't always your friend either!

But if the actual thoughts are about indifference and negativity, can you predict what you might get fused to? How is your mind going to mess with you? What will your negative self-talk be when you engage in these actions? Will it be Old Home Week with you telling yourself the same denigrating comments? What has this "broken record" been saying that distracts—or even stops you—from moving forward successfully toward your desired goal? Record those thoughts below.

_____

_____

_____

_____

_____

Pick the knottiest of the phrases from that list and then grab an index card or a slip of paper that you can carry in your wallet or purse. As you write the troublesome phrase (or phrases) on your paper, follow these instructions:

Write the phrase with odd spacing between some of the letters and words.

Smush some words together, and awkwardly separate some of the letters.

Write a letter backward and capitalize a few in the middle of the word.

For instance, if you believe that one of your cognitive obstacles is going to be "I can't do this because I'm a failure," then write it this way:

IcA ntdoTh is be CausEima? Ail ure.

Now go ahead and put the paper with your phrase in your handbag or wallet so you'll occasionally see it. Take a picture of it and use it as your smartphone home screen. When you see it, view it as silly squiggles and lines that quite obviously have no sway over what you do with your life. In many ways, this will simply remind you that the obstacle you *believe* will impede you from keeping your commitments actually can be viewed differently and distantly. This will weaken your attachment to the phrase and loosen up the influence the thoughts have on you.

Now, in order to truly make your MAP impactful, write these knotty phrases directly in the Noticing section. This will help remind you of the obstacle, but also help you to take a distant view of that kind of thinking.

We've weakened the grip that thoughts have by "deliteralizing" the language and viewing the thoughts differently. When you're no longer in their grasp, you can change how you behave. Now let's do an exercise to observe how weak language can be when compared to the strength of action.

DETACH FROM THOUGHTS

Wiggle your toes. Truly do this action and commit to wiggle them for one minute. Now read this carefully: I cannot wiggle my toes. Did that sentence you just read affect your commitment? If not, you're demonstrating noticing; if so, you were fused!

Let's continue. The clock is still ticking on the one minute, so hopefully you're still keeping the wiggling commitment. Now read this again, but continue with mindful action: I cannot wiggle my toes. Say that phrase again to yourself with your eyes closed. Make it a thought: *I cannot wiggle my toes.* Did you experience yourself noticing the words, but *not* having your actions attached to them? It's like experiencing an irony: you say you can't do something, and then prove to yourself that you actually can! Now that your one minute is up, let's do another one.

Commit to maintaining silence for thirty seconds. Now read this: I have to clear my throat. Recall your commitment to stay silent, and notice the presence of that phrase. Now repeat this to yourself with your eyes closed so that it's a thought: *I have to clear my throat.* Read it again and observe if you're actually getting an urge to cough or swallow hard. Now, to show the power of words and how it will change the way you feel, say the phrase out loud: "I have to clear my throat." If you followed those written instructions, you were fused to the language on this page! If you uttered those six words even though you committed to maintaining silence for thirty seconds, you weren't noticing language; you were governed by it. However, if you stayed silent the whole time you were reading this passage, you're demonstrating noticing language because the thirty seconds is up.

Wiggling your toes when you think you can't and not clearing your throat when you tell yourself you have to do so are lighthearted examples demonstrating that your actions can be detached from your thoughts. More practically, when you commit to doing what you care about, your thoughts have the potential of getting in the way of moving forward, but you can dispassionately pass by such obstacles by noticing their presence instead of becoming attached to them.

Now let's look at detachment from thoughts using another perspective. You've been absorbing information from this book for a while, thereby demonstrating you're proficient with the skill of reading. You're doing it fluently and successfully. Now imagine explaining how to read. During this explanation, articulate exactly how you do this skill as completely as possible so someone who is illiterate can understand how to do this action. Of course, this is an impossible task, but it makes a point about how doing some actions can be detached from thinking. For many committed actions, your mind doesn't have to coach you through all the steps. *You do it!* You don't have to think about it. You already do many things with a solid degree of acumen without having to let your mind's extra descriptions, evaluations, and problem-solving get involved, so give that a whirl when you're finding yourself stymied by your own thoughts. As the Latin phrase intones, *acta non verba,* or "actions not words," implying that engaging in measurable behavior is more important than the talking that goes on around it. There are times to treat thoughts as disconnected from values-based behavior.

Noticing's Caveat

There's a caveat to all of this detaching and thought noticing: you *can* choose to let words have an impact on you! It'd be ridiculous to ask you to *only* notice *all* your thoughts! Some describing, evaluating, and problem-solving are critical to get us through the day. More importantly, the language of your values is crucial to a life well lived. When you did your values clarification exercises in chapter 4, and when you continually fill in What I Care About on the MAP, such language can be embraced as meaningful and impactful.

● *Ali's Story*

Ali was given the opportunity to see her company's executive coach. The coach encouraged Ali to practice mindfulness and noticing with her problematic thoughts related to her own abilities, the world, and the future. The coach invited her to see these thoughts as if they were on a teleprompter on a train platform, and to just watch the form of those thoughts scroll by as if they were just a bunch of squiggles and lines. But the coach also helped Ali clarify what she cared about and discussed that these values—this language—can hold sway over her actions because they support a life well lived. Ali learned that language is a curse and a gift, and she could choose to distance herself from the blight of obstructive words, and to allow values-based words to be a blessing while leveraging those words to encourage vitality into her actions. She was able to say, "I am here now, accepting the stress and strain of this middle-management job, noticing my thoughts related to self-denigration and being pessimistic about the world and the future, while demonstrating leadership and creativity because I care about improving the quality of life for other people, about safety, and about being a good provider."

Moving Forward

Psychological flexibility and mindful action are about actively choosing how you respond under different circumstances. You undermine unhelpful language processes by noticing when they occur, and leverage your own values-based language to help you take action toward what is most important. Now you have a few more tools to help you stay focused on doing what you care about in the here and now rather than being stopped by the obstacles your own thoughts place on your path. You've learned about contacting the present moment and how to accept your feelings as a natural part of the journey of doing what you care about, and embraced some ways to let go of unsupportive thoughts rather than getting hooked into believing everything your mind tells you. We'll turn now to the final skill set for mindful action—examining who's doing all this work of accepting, noticing, and being here now: your *self*!

CHAPTER 9

I Am

We round out our chapters going through the sections of the Mindful Action Plan by returning to the starting point of the MAP: *I am* here now, accepting the way I feel, noticing my thoughts, while doing what I care about. The journey of becoming who you want to be—how you want to be in the world and doing what you care about—can be facilitated with the skills you're learning throughout this book. The MAP adds another skill encouraging you to relate to the way you think about your "self" differently.

A Piece of the MAP: I Am

| I Am | Observe if you are being influenced by any unhelpful self-descriptions. Let go of any problematic thoughts you are believing about your self. | |

As you engage in your mindful actions, observe how you're being influenced by any unhelpful self-descriptions. The MAP encourages letting go of any problematic thoughts you believe about your self. You've already practiced accepting feelings and noticing thoughts in chapters 7 and 8. In this chapter, you apply those skills to your thoughts about *yourself*—the stories and labels you developed throughout your life about who you are, what you're capable of, and what defines you. You'll also come into contact with a centered core self. You can observe your languaging as a kind of behavior just like thinking or talking or walking: you also engage in "self-ing." Acceptance and commitment therapy refers to such skills as "self-as-context" (which we'll be talking more specifically about a bit later in this chapter), and on the MAP, it's known as the I Am experience.

Most people don't spend long periods of time in self-reflection, writing autobiographies or journaling extensively about life's experiences, but we all have our stories about who we are. Over the course of our lives, we develop a sense of "self"—a "self-concept"—through our interactions with others and with our environment, and ultimately through our own use of language. We compare ourselves to others, categorize ourselves as belonging to various groups, identify as having assorted roles, and describe ourselves as being like or different from other people in our lives. You made some notes about the stories you tell about yourself in chapter 2, and the MAP asks you to notice the influence of your self-descriptions. Let's continue this exploration with the following exercise.

Exercise: I Am…

For this exercise, you will need four blank pieces of paper.

At the top of the first page, write the phrase "I am _____." Set a timer for one minute and write all the self-descriptions that come to you. When the timer ends, set the paper aside.

Now at the top of another page, write the phrase "I am not _____." Again, set a timer for one minute and write all the self-descriptions that come to you. When the timer ends, set the paper aside.

At the top of another page, write the phrase "I am able to _____." Again, set a timer for one minute and write all the self-descriptions that come to you. When the timer ends, set the paper aside.

Finally, at the top of another page, write the phrase "I am unable to _____." Again, set a timer for one minute and write all the self-descriptions that come to you. When the timer ends, set the paper aside.

Sit for a moment with all of the pages in front of you. You've created a portrait of yourself with words. What do you see? How many of these words categorize you within a group? How many describe you as being different from others? How many of these statements involve evaluations of yourself? How many are positive? How many are critical? Do some contradict others?

Have you captured absolutely everything about yourself? If someone were to look at these pages, would they know everything there is to know about you? We guess the answer to that question is no, of course not! Our evaluations and descriptions of ourselves are endless. A single label or even four pages of labels can't define us or capture every aspect of our experiences and qualities. We'll come back to this "self-portrait" in a little bit, but for now, just sit with the feelings and thoughts arising from this exercise and note them below.

_____

_____

_____

Seeing Our Stories

When we were at work on this book, at different times we found ourselves stuck in unhelpful self-criticism and doubt—as many authors experience. Siri found herself freezing as she set out to write, and having the thought *I am not an ACT person!* screaming loudly in her mind. As a behavior analyst and coach, not a therapist, she had convinced herself that DJ would see her as a fraud when it came to knowing about all this ACT stuff—despite having spent more than a decade using ACT for herself and within her practice, and having a PhD in relational frame theory (the theoretical, scientific foundation for ACT). The funny thing is, DJ was saying to himself, *I'm not being scientific enough with my writing, and Siri will think I don't understand relational frame theory very well.* We all get wrapped up in our own self-talk at times, and the MAP helps us untangle ourselves.

These kinds of statements—like the phrases you wrote down in the last exercise—can function as "rules" we follow without thinking. As we mentioned briefly in the last chapter, self-talk can be helpful—providing reminders of how to act in line with our values or prompting us to do things we care about in small ways. Athletes might tell themselves rules to remember to engage in particular actions, like a surfer using self-talk for staying balanced in the sweet spot of the surfboard, and ensuring their paddling strokes are deep in the water to build enough speed to catch the wave. "Self-rules" like these can also include reminders of our values and actions like "I'm prioritizing my sleep so that I'm well rested for teaching tomorrow, and I won't drink wine after dinner." Talking to yourself about your actions and values, as well as your capabilities and qualities, can be a source of resilience and strength. Your self-rules guide action toward meaningful activities. The Mindful Action Plan itself begins with a self-rule: "I am here now, accepting the way I feel, noticing my thoughts, while doing what I care about." However, the rules we tell ourselves can also create hindrances—obstacles on our path—impeding the actions we care about.

Self-rules can be particularly problematic when they lead you to avoid valuable circumstances and toward negative self-evaluations. Your self-concepts are rooted in your *past* experiences, which are fixed and static and can't be changed, and yet you have the potential to be flexible in the current moment. Rigidly adhering to our own rules about what we can and can't do leaves us little room for growth. If someone has the rule "I am awkward and I can't speak well in public" because their first experiences with public speaking (like most people's) was difficult, they might avoid career paths that might have been interesting and values-based. If Siri was stuck in "I am not an ACT person" because her background is different from ACT therapists, she might have turned down the offer to write this book, and then where would we all be?! Psychological flexibility requires holding our ideas about ourselves lightly—as simply words, not truths, and therefore as changeable, not fixed. In the last chapter, we discussed some ways to notice these kinds of obstacles, and those tools are also useful when we talk about ourselves. Siri could sing her negative self-evaluation, write it backward on her MAP, or use any of the many other ways to pull the power out of the words—to defuse them from her actions. When it comes to language about our "self," though, sometimes more is needed—after all, we are very important to ourselves, so it's hard to just "let go" of language that feels somehow essential to our very being.

Senses of Self-ing

From an acceptance and commitment therapy point of view, there are three main ways that we use language about our self, and all can be helpful or unhelpful, depending on the situation. One of the ways we create our self-concept is through stories and descriptions about who we are in the sense of the roles we play and the qualities we see as defining us. For instance, Siri identifies as a mother, a behavior analyst, kind and compassionate, a teacher, and able to be patient and tolerant—although her child may disagree! She can also identify as someone who is a worrier, not spontaneous, unable to handle crowds and noise, and on and on. DJ identifies as a dad, a consultant, gritty and adventurous, a runner, and funny—although lots of people disagree! We can call this type of language behavior *self-as-content*: we define ourselves by the *content* of our experiences and what others have told us about who we are.

Another way we construct our "self" involves identifying what we're feeling and doing in this moment—Siri and DJ could both say, "I am tired," "I am distracted," "I am worried." Or, at other times, "I am excited," "I am focused," "I am typing words for this book," etc. We call this type of language behavior *self-as-process*: we're identifying what's going on with the self in this moment in time and in the *process* of experiencing.

A final way we create our self-concept is witnessing the self—observing "my self" as a person who is observing. This is the sense of the self that is a constant perspective from which you observe that you are a runner or a teacher (content), and tired or excited (processes). This is called *self-as-context*, and the *context* is holding the content and processes. It's tricky to put into words because it's highly experiential, so we're going to come back to this with an exercise later in the chapter.

Each of these ways of self-ing is valuable. The more flexible we can become with our language in each of these patterns, the more we'll act in alignment with our values, even when the situation changes dramatically. Take your time with the following exercise to reflect on the ways your own self-talk might be helpful or create an obstacle.

EXERCISE: Linking the Self to Action

Return to the self-portrait you created with the four sheets of paper. What rules and stories can you identify in those statements?

- Circle the ones that are related to the "content" of your experience.

- Put a box around the ones that are related to the "process" of experiencing.

How many of them reflect a past "you" in past circumstances that might no longer apply in the present? How might it be helpful to let go of any of that self-ing in order for you to become more psychologically flexible and engage in your values-based commitments?

Consider a domain on your Life Atlas and a related action on your to-do list that you struggle with. How might your self-rules be presenting an obstacle to doing what you care about? Work that out below.

Doing/What I Care About: _____

Related I Am statements: _____

Are these descriptions of "content" or "process"? Are they relevant to your current circumstances?

_____

_____

_____

_____

Which of these help you progress on your path?

_____

_____

_____

_____

Which of these present obstacles on your path?

_____

_____

_____

_____

If you mindfully noticed these self-descriptions, how would that change your actions?

_____

_____

_____

_____

Letting Go: Rewriting Our Stories

In the last exercise, you may have expressed the stories you tell about yourself that are helpful, but in other circumstances, those same stories present obstacles. Becoming more psychologically flexible means you're building skills in shifting how you relate to your stories within the given context so you can recognize when they're unhelpful and let them go, or just put them away momentarily, making space for them in your backpack as you journey on your chosen path. You can repeatedly rewrite the stories, but there are many ways that your own language, as well as the language of others and your larger context—your family, the groups you're a part of, your cultural background, and current iden-tification—gets you inflexibly stuck in your stories.

Some of the ways we get stuck are inherent problems of how language works, which we've talked about in various ways in every chapter of this book. We get fused to our words and like it when our stories are familiar and predictable, whether we created those rules ourselves or they've been given to

.us by others. We try to make sense of our circumstances by fitting them to our existing stories about ourselves. For instance, if someone avoids public speaking for years but then is suddenly thrust into the spotlight and doesn't perform perfectly, they're likely to ascribe the poor performance to their inherent weakness as a public speaker—blaming their own self rather than ascribing their performance to lack of practice and the challenging and unexpected situation.

However, it's not just our own language tendencies that throw obstacles in our path. It's also the language of others in our context. The culture at large often teaches us inappropriate and unattainable ideals about what it means to be worthy. We're conditioned to have rules of what it means to be productive, successful, a "good parent," attractive, and on and on. An individual who identifies as nonbinary often can't even find language to fit their identity. For instance, what is a gender-neutral term for "niece/nephew" that everyone would understand? This lack of language reinforces thinking that they are in a world "not made for them" and then creates self-talk that they're stuck with "awkward phrasing because I'm an awkward person." Single fathers and stay-at-home dads find themselves depicted as similarly "lesser than" or "invisible" in much of society's messages and advertising, and many women might find themselves characterized as "snooty" or "bitchy" if they set boundaries with male colleagues by simply refusing to always be the one to take notes in a meeting.

Everyone in our society finds it hard to be continually compared to narrowly defined roles and ideals. No wonder our own self-talk is so frequently negative! Moreover, society often sticks us with singular, simplistic labels—whether that's completely defining someone by their gender, role as a parent or partner, disability, weight, physical appearance, and so on. Return to the many statements you wrote about yourself in earlier exercises. As we asked before, would any single one of these statements capture who you are? Of course not! Getting stuck in a label is another way your language stops you dead in your tracks while on your valued journey.

Let's look at some ways we can get unstuck—some ways you can "let go of any problematic thoughts you believe about yourself."

Making Space for Variability

In chapter 7, you did some exercises to improve your self-observation skills—noticing your own thoughts and accepting your internal physical and emotional experiences. You may have noticed a wide range of experiences even in just a few days of practice. Think back over the past month, the past year, the past decade. Are you "the same person" now as you were then? Do you respond the exact same way? Do you have the exact same feelings? Observing the variability of your experiences helps you see that you're not a fixed, static entity—you feel different feelings and engage in different actions, depending on the context. Since your context is always changing, you have the capacity to change along with it.

As Siri thought about her own self-rules, she realized that while she wasn't the same kind of "ACT person" her own therapist was, and although when she began her career, she didn't know anything about ACT, she indeed had gained a wealth of knowledge and experience with ACT over the years. She could confidently say, "I'm not *that* kind of ACT person [referring to therapists in general], *and* I am my own kind of ACT person." She also realized that some days she indeed could be "too tired" or overwhelmed, while on other days she wasn't. In addition, through ACT, she learned she could also be overwhelmed *and* be a teacher, a writer, a parent, a partner. She learned to shift what actions she committed to each day in light of the context that day presented, allowing for variability in her goals and actions so long as they were still at least inching forward in the direction of her values. Some days that meant parenting took priority, and she had to make space for the variability of that experience as well—after all, it's a very different thing to be a "good mother" to a teenager than to a toddler.

Return to the statements you wrote previously. What self-talk have you identified about who you are and what you're capable of? What roles and labels have defined you previously? Experiment with adding cues for yourself like "I am _____ *and* _____" or "I am *sometimes* _____ *and* I am sometimes _____." How can you remind yourself to make space for the range of human experience?

I am _____ and _____.

I am _____ and _____.

I am sometimes _____ and sometimes _____.

I am sometimes _____ and sometimes _____.

Recall how much changes with your own individual experiences over the course of a day, a week, a year, a lifetime. Make some notes about this below and in the I Am section of your MAP.

_____

_____

_____

Seeing Yourself from Another Point of View

Everyone operates from the perspective of "I am here now." When I stand "here," "here" can't ever be "there," for once I go "there," "there" becomes "here." Additionally, "now" can't ever be "then," and "I" can't be "you." The MAP starts out saying "I am here now" in order to focus on yourself and center your experience on the current moment. This is foundational to mindful action.

Alternatively, if you use language flexibly, you can observe yourself from other perspectives. You can see yourself as you are here and now as different from the way you were there and then. For instance, your language assists with remembering the roles you had ten years ago compared to the roles you have now; witnessing your ability to have such change can support your efforts in further change. In the "Be Kind to Yourself" section from chapter 7, we discussed self-compassion and invited you to treat yourself with the kindness you show to another person you care about. Seeing yourself from another perspective is also a powerful way to make space for different self-talk, and it engenders increased flexibility. Let's try another way of perspective taking now.

Taking the Kind Coach Perspective

Review your "I am" statements from earlier exercises. Is this how you think your best friend would describe you? Your mother? A loved one? Take a moment and imagine how a trusted friend would describe you. Write what you think that person would say about you. If it might be helpful to your committed actions, can you try on any of these statements as a new self-rule? What would the next week be like if you followed that rule?

_____

_____

_____

_____

_____

Think back to your "self" of five years ago. Do you have any kind words of advice to that self? How might you describe that "past you" from your perspective now?

_____

_____

_____

_____

Imagine yourself five years from now, looking back with kindness and compassion on the "you" of today. How might "future you" describe "current you"? Can you imagine any kind words of advice for "current you"?

_____

_____

_____

_____

Look again at your MAP. Can you see space for a new perspective in the I Am section that could help you move forward on your path? Jot such reminders on the MAP.

Making Space for Growth

Ultimately, all the exercises in this workbook are about growth and about trying on new ways of being and acting in the world that get you further down your valued path. The more you can see yourself as the "container" for all your experiences, the better you can see how individual experiences don't have to define you. Repeat the Whitman quote, "I am large, I contain multitudes." You are bigger than your experiences, and you are bigger than the labels you and others place on yourself. You have the capacity to contain both successes and mistakes, as well as actions congruent with your values and also those you regret. Just as your language presents you with obstacles, like getting stuck in the story of a failure, you can use your skills to notice those obstacles and continue journeying on your path.

Consider a domain of your Life Atlas and a related action on your to-do list where you're struggling, and reflect on all the self-statements you've been observing. Are there any "I am" statements reflecting past mistakes, regrets, or worries that might present an obstacle for you? Now, try taking different perspectives on some of the concerns you've been wrestling with. Review any of the past issues that give you some trepidation about moving forward—perhaps your mistakes, regrets, or worries that haunt you and impede valued action.

I made a mistake when _____, and from that experience I benefited

because _____.

I regret when _____, and because of that unfortunate

experience, I _____.

I worry about _____, and I can hold that feeling while still moving

forward with _____.

In what ways can you make space for growth, learn from the past, and do what you care about now? Make some notes about this below and in the I Am section of your MAP.

_____

_____

_____

_____

Getting Flexible

Look at all the phrases and stories you've written about yourself. As you become more self-observant, you begin to practice more flexible ways of talking about yourself—seeing *you* as the *context* for all your experiences. This way of "self-ing" has many names, and in the ACT community it has been called the "transcendent sense of self." When you take this view, you speak from the point of "I am here now" as an unchanging and continuous perspective over time, even as the events of your life change and your sense of who you are evolves. This can be an advantageous perspective to take, especially in times of drastic change. For instance, at one point, DJ was married, living with his two high school–aged children in a small town in the Midwest, and running a clinic he founded. In a year's time, he was a divorced empty-nester, living by the ocean and working as a professor. Having a sense of a strong, steadfast self was crucial for dealing with the chaotic and emotionally difficult changes in a psychologically flexible manner. We all have something unbroken, unchanged, and forming a cohesive whole that we discover in tumultuous life experiences: a transcendent sense of self! There is a core you—the *I am* experience—that provides an unwavering context holding all your impermanent content and life's inevitable processes.

This transcendent sense of self develops by being the observer of your own experiences while also being the one who is observed. It's the self-compassionate experience of being the caretaker, while also being the one being taken care of. In the following exercise, you will practice shifting between seeing the content of your experiences and seeing yourself as the context of those experiences.

EXAMINING THE FIBER OF YOUR BEING

For this exercise, you will need two chairs, a spool of yarn, a pen, and either index cards and paper clips or sticky notes. You'll need to be in a space where you can stretch out the yarn. Begin by recalling major events that happened in your life—births, deaths, graduations, starting a new job, moves, marriage, divorce, and so on. Write a few words about each event on the card or note. Recall other moments that had a great impact on you—the first time someone said "I love you" or when someone did something kind when you needed it, and write these down too.

Take the yarn and tie the end of it to a chair on one side of the room, and then unspool it to form something like a clothesline, looping it around the other chair, and letting the remainder of the yarn rest on the floor. Place the cards describing your events along the line in chronological order with the end tied to the first chair representing your birth, and the loop around the other chair representing this present moment. Spend time truly revisiting each event, describing it in detail.

Now stand at the final point on your timeline. As you look down the line, notice the connection between the moment you were born and now. Take a different perspective, and stand back from the line looking at it as the content of your life. Then return to the "now" by holding the yarn up to your nose, and observe the continuous line is *you*, the very fiber your own life, the cord of your own existence. You can look at the yarn and see it exists and connects to all these events. You are represented by this strand. A core you exists and connects to all you have encountered and experienced.

Also notice the remaining spool of yarn, and how this core you will continue into the future, regardless of the events that inevitably get placed upon the line. Aim to put the elements of your to-do list and how you want to live on that cord going forward. Take a moment to sit with this experience and make a few notes before returning to the chapter.

_____

_____

_____

_____

_____

Shifting between the experiences of "self-as content" (looking at the notes) and "self-as-context" (looking down the yarn) is a useful way to increase your psychological flexibility. As Siri sat with this exercise, she was able to see the different aspects of her experiences as shaping her life while still remaining uniquely "herself." She made space for the thought that she was "not an ACT person," while also making space for the ways in which she brought ACT into her work in her own way. She made note of these on her MAP, and found renewed energy and commitment to the task of writing this book. She also found it easier to accept her feelings of vulnerability and anxiety about her contributions, realizing that, of course, she didn't know everything there was to possibly know about ACT, and that was okay. She recognized that the process of writing could also be a process of learning and growing, and that her contributions were valuable in their own way—her sense of self expanded to contain all of these experiences, thoughts, and feelings about her work. Her MAP phrase read, "I am here now, accepting my feelings of vulnerability, noticing my thoughts about myself and my lack of experience, while doing what I care about."

As another example of self-examination, DJ's fortunate training in ACT was beneficial when experiencing the aforementioned life changes in a brief period of time. For a large portion of adulthood, he said, "I am married," "I am a homeowner," "I am from a small town," "I am a Midwesterner," and "I am fortunate to live with my kids." Within a year, those self-descriptions no longer fit. But examine each one of his phrases. Observe that a small yet critical part of each of those self-descriptions remained: *I am*. Being able to witness the immutable foundation holding together those past experiences, and recognizing that this transcendent sense of self continued to be *foundational* for the present experiences, provided the support for mindful actions to occur, even though DJ's surrounding world had changed irrevocably. His MAP phrase read, "I am here now, accepting my feelings of grief and newfound happiness, noticing my thoughts of regret and hopefulness, while moving forward with my life while carrying the same—yet more clarified—values."

When *you* can see your *self* as the continuous, unchanging line throughout your life events, you begin to see your self as *containing* the wide variety of your experiences, rather than as being *defined* by any single one. Such a perspective can help you be more self-compassionate, secure, and psychologically flexible. It may also allow you to see your "stories" as just that—language you've been conditioned to use—rather than being fixed, true rules you must adhere to. Plan to shift into this "observer" perspective regularly as you practice noticing your thoughts and accepting your feelings throughout your day as you engage in mindful action.

Moving Forward

As you worked through this chapter addressing the I Am component of the MAP, you practiced making space for rules and stories you have about yourself that might be causing a barrier to doing what you care about. This added another set of skills to improve your psychological flexibility. In earlier chapters, you improved your ability to accept feelings, notice thoughts, and let go of obstacles to doing what you care about in the present moment. Now you're developing skills to do so when thoughts and feelings are about your *self*. That's a really hard thing to do! Check in regularly with the I Am section on your MAP. Observe your own self and see it expanding to include all of your new skills, and see how it generates progress with your committed actions. We'll wrap up *all* the skills you've learned so far in the next and final chapter.

CHAPTER 10

The MAP: A Global View

You are here! You've found your why and found your way to the end of the book and to a clearer path ahead. Of course, you'll never be done with clarifying your values and committing to act in ways that bring meaning and purpose to your life. Your journey will evolve as you grow and as new circumstances present challenges and opportunities. But now you have a whole set of orienteering skills when you get lost or stuck. In this final chapter, we'll return to a global view of your MAP and your Life Atlas. While we've been discussing each of the elements of the MAP as separate skills, they truly integrate together to embolden and enable mindful action.

Reviewing the MAP

While walking through each step of the MAP, you familiarized yourself with interrelated skills strengthening psychological flexibility. Psychological flexibility is associated with increased quality of living, reduction in suffering, and improved well-being, and these outcomes are observed in the contexts of work, education, relationships, personal growth and health (physical and behavioral), and leisure. Mindful action is an overt display of psychological flexibility, and the Mindful Action Plan is a powerful, practical tool for creating a life well lived.

The MAP supports how you organize your time and efforts each day on your journey in life. As recommended in chapter 1, print out these tools, affix them to a clipboard, and keep them at-the-ready in different contexts of your life. Place a MAP clipboard where you eat breakfast so it facilitates planning your day, and hang one on your wall where you work to accelerate higher performance. Having these readily available not only keeps you focused on your to-do list, but also strengthens and integrates the skills that support your values-based behaviors.

Each element of the MAP adds interwoven layers of skills to your backpack as you travel your chosen path, assisting in effectively carrying all your experiences and emotions, even the heavy ones. The MAP elements can be viewed as two interconnected categories of skills that are central to ACT. The first four elements—I Am, Here Now, Accepting (the way I feel), Noticing (my thoughts)—can be thought of as broadly promoting *mindfulness*. The second two elements (including the performance management section)—Doing-What I Care About—are the essence of valued and committed *action*. Put them together, and we have *mindful action*. In chapter 1, we defined mindful action as purposeful, present-focused, committed behavior that you do while maximally attending to what you choose to make important, unhindered by distractions. More specifically, recall that mindful action is:

- *fully committed to achieving a goal,*
- done with *full awareness of what one is doing*
- while aiming to *be more reliably in the here and now*, and
- engaged in *action in the direction of what you care about*
- by *focusing most of your attention on what you choose to be important in your life,*
- not stopped by *obstacles within the human condition*
- by building psychological skills through *a context supporting the practice of mindfulness.*

In this definition, you see how elements of the MAP integrate with each other to guide you toward doing more of what you care about. For instance, you might use some of the Noticing strategies you learned in chapter 8 to release unhelpful self-descriptions so you can embrace the I Am experience (chapter 9). Clarifying your values and What I Care About (chapter 4) helps dignify the pain of Accepting painful emotions, as you learned to do in chapter 7. You might use some micropractices to help you stay Here Now as you learned about in chapter 6 to support your ability to maximally attend to Doing your committed actions that you listed in chapter 5. You will find that certain goals or actions require more of these skills than others and in unique combinations. There's no one set "right" way to use the MAP. Because it's a tool for psychological flexibility, it's inherently flexible. To exemplify the many possible ways you can use all the elements of the MAP together, let's return to the individual journeys of the people we've been following in each chapter.

● Ella's Journey

After she spent some time really clarifying her values, Ella reoriented her education and career goals. Shifting from pediatrics to emergency room nursing breathed new life into her commitment to school activities. She is also finding more harmony as she spends a "better for her" balance of time among friendships, health-related activities, and education. But she still grapples with talking to her parents about her choices. Even though she identified relevant values, she needs something more to follow through on her commitment to communicate with them. Her deep fear of rejection and disapproval—a big but natural emotion—shows up every time she thinks about the upcoming conversation, along with critical self-talk about being ungrateful. She does the "Kind Coach" exercise with this in mind, commits to her regular mindfulness practices to help support her in maintaining a "transcendent sense of self" perspective, and plans to spend time noticing the environment around her before she steps through the door of her parents' house. She also tells her best friend that she's going to talk to her parents and adds a reward—a weekend brunch date with her friend—to her performance management contract for this task. Ella feels like she's on her way to truly carving out a path that works for her.

● Ken's Journey

The Ironman was excruciatingly difficult, but Ken met the challenge. He completed the world-class endurance event, and did so with Shannon's coaching and the MAP's guidance. One contributing factor to his success was genuinely implementing mindful practices. Ken embraced Shannon's advice to meditate, and realized he was wrong to think that the mindfulness exercises were nonsensically taking time away from physical exercises. He dropped his skepticism when he started to comprehend how mindfulness enhanced his fitness, his endurance, and, most importantly, his commitment to doing the workouts.

Mindfulness won't help you get to the finish line unless you also use it to get to the starting line. Ken embraced meditation's effectiveness for staying dedicated to what he cared about, especially on days that the prep work was particularly grueling and came at an inopportune time in his calendar. He more clearly saw that all his preparations for the Ironman were linked to his values related to his health and the nonprofits he supported. When he'd tell himself that he was too busy with after-work job tasks to do his training, he defused from such thoughts, and was inspired to exercise because he linked such efforts to purposefully having an impact on people being helped by the charities. When the complaining thoughts weren't obvious to him, but he still didn't feel like exercising, he accepted that emotional state, and willingly carried it with him as he laced up for a training run. Shannon suggested that he be judicious with sensations and feelings because fatigue can be a sign of overtraining, but also told him to not let such feelings be dictators bullying him to not follow through on what he cared about. She also made sure to leverage the power of reinforcement by having Ken create authentic performance management incentives to keep him—and the fancy socks—on his toes.

The Tiptons' Journey

Ron's stressed-out mom and dad clarified their why for parenting: rearing Ron to have a full, healthy, enjoyable life. They also learned the skills of parent management training, and embraced the mindfulness exercises the pediatric professional taught them for supplementing their commitment to the treatment plan.

By mutually supporting each other in doing traditional mindfulness exercises as well as impromptu micropractices, the couple became more fluent in contacting the present moment. They even listened to guided meditations together to support their mindful parenting, but then something else happened: their mindfulness skills started to generalize. More frequently they found that they were present in the moment (here now) when other challenges came up. The couple stopped putting off the housekeeping chores and the yard work because they were more judicious with how they spent their time. Being in the here and now influenced them to deal with paying their bills on time, folding the laundry instead of procrastinating until it piled too high, and then, most importantly, showing love and kindness to each other, realizing that now is the only time you can do anything important.

Cal's Journey

Cal's been doing well with their art production goals. They've also built skills for accepting how much it just sucks to step into the studio some days, but doing it anyway. However, when they started to take a look at other aspects of their life, they realized they still had work to do. Like the

Tiptons, as much as Cal loved their kids, Cal realized that they weren't often enjoying simply being present with the kids. All that cooking was probably functioning, at least in part, to avoid those same feelings and thoughts showing up first around creating art, but then also about being a selfish single parent. For this aspect of their life, though, a focus on staying in the here and now was what was needed, in combination with the acceptance skills they'd been practicing. Cal made some notes in the I Am section of their MAP (in glitter pen!), committed to activities they would do with the kids, and planned mindful exercises to do before the kids got home from school, then promised themself to engage in micropractices throughout the evening when they felt themself getting distracted. As Cal shifts more energy into the domain of parenting, they start to feel a shift in overall harmony and find themself enjoying time in the studio as well as time with the kids in a deeper way.

● Ali's Journey

Leading people to behave more safely within an entrenched work culture continued to be stressful for Ali, but she aimed to have her values prevail. In the presence of anxiety, she learned to accept the aversive feeling, and interact with fellow employees in an effective manner anyway. With all the self-criticism and hopeless thoughts, Ali began to relate to these thoughts differently, noticing that they just kept appearing throughout the day, but that the thoughts didn't need to govern her actions. She committed to reading more about safety management and leadership skills, and relied on her values to help her generate further motivation to bring the best out in herself and other people at the mill.

Ali would start the workday by centering and grounding herself first, and take a moment to engage with her self-as-context. It was at that point that she would then sit at her desk, print out a MAP, post it on her clipboard, and begin to review her job tasks. She always had a lot to do, but she learned to prioritize with the four quadrants and then flexibly manage her objectives for the day. She quickly recalled the self-denigrating thoughts that beleaguered her throughout the day, and took a breath and imagined them as if those words were painted on posters being carried by toy soldiers in a parade. She watched them march on by, distant from her, as if they were just sterile squiggles and lines. And then she stood up with her to-do list, marched her steel-toed boots out to the manufacturing room floor, and started making a leadership impact on the mill's safety culture.

● Siri and DJ's Journeys

This book you're holding is the end result of our work on our own Mindful Action Plans! Different points in the process of writing called for different strategies—some aspects were tedious, some frustrating, and both defusion and acceptance strategies were necessary, as well as plenty of performance management. (DJ benefited from Siri being his accountability partner for some of that.) Of course, each of us also had a lot of "life" going on around us. Both of us had to make sure that our focus on this book and other projects wasn't unduly taking away from our relationships with our kids, partners, and friends—even though all of them recognized that we were committed to spending time in this valued professional domain. Siri purposefully made time to be present with her kid, reminding herself that they would be off to college really soon—but Siri really needed to work on the "being present" part of that. DJ saw this book project as a vehicle to reduce suffering and improve quality of living for people, and aimed to let that value motivate his mindful action, especially on days when he didn't feel like writing. He accepted these feelings willingly and committed to generating the necessary keystrokes. Bottom line: we all struggle! We utilized the MAP as a critical planning tool, and as much as we'd like it to be, it isn't a magic wand! Engaging in mindful action planning is an ongoing, sometimes painful but ultimately rewarding process.

Mindful Action Planning for Continual Improvement

As each of the above examples illustrates, the MAP is best used as a continually evolving tool for self-reflection that enables you to focus on doing the activities that bring meaning and purpose to your life. Progress on your Life Atlas will be incremental, and mindful action will support continuous, gradual improvement. As you've been using the MAP throughout this book, we hope you've had a chance to think deeply about what's getting done and not getting done on your to-do list. Are you using the MAP to do more of what you care about, and less of what you don't? How do you feel when you're engaged in the activities you set out to do? Fundamentally, how's your journey going, and are you moving forward?

In chapter 5, we suggested that you consider your to-do list in terms of what valued areas of your life are getting more or less attention. Let's return now to the Life Atlas exercise from chapter 3 to reconsider how close you are to journeying on your chosen path, and how well you're able to travel between the domains of your life. Begin by considering whether the domains you initially identified sufficiently capture what's important to you now that you've had more time to consider your values and activities. If you'd like to edit these, take some time to do that now. Then, returning to the work you've done throughout this book, particularly in chapter 4, reflect on your values in each of these domains. Now that you've more thoroughly explored what mindful action is throughout this workbook, shape your values statements to be more precise and authentic as they relate to finding your why.

Domain: _____

Values: _____

_____

Domain: _____

Values: _____

_____

Domain: _____

Values: _____

_____

Domain: _____

Values: _____

_____

Domain: _____

Values: _____

_____

Taking a blank version of the Life Atlas (which you can download at http://www.newharbinger .com/50713), reflect on the MAPs you've been working with throughout this book and identify where you currently are on your path in each domain. Are you feeling lost, or stuck, or are you meaningfully moving forward on your valued path?

And now, reflect on the big picture—how are you feeling about the harmony between the domains of your life? Again, these might not be evenly balanced, but we're aiming for harmony among these domains, not perfect equality. How workable are they for this moment in time?

For the domains where all is well, great job! Keep it up! Enjoy the scenery of the path you're on—try not to get too caught up in always looking ahead to achieving the next goal. For domains where you're feeling lost, think about what wayfinding tools might help you orient yourself and move forward. Would it be helpful to reassess whether the actions you have on your list are aligned with the values you identified? Look at what you're doing that competes with doing your written goals, and investigate if those actions are actually in line with other values, or if they're problematic and leading to insidious short-term rewards. Perhaps your chosen actions might fit better with an altered, more clarified value (like Siri discovered with her swimming goal in chapter 4). Are there external barriers that you could address with the performance management strategies from chapter 5? Could the action itself be broken down more into smaller steps, or could your goal be articulated more clearly— making it a SMARTER and WISE goal? Or are the barriers arising because you're caught up in there-then thinking, unwilling to accept your emotions, unable to notice your thoughts, and wrapped up in obstructive self-talk? Work through chapters 6 to 9 again while focusing on this domain.

If you feel far from your path for some domains, it's likely you feel like the bigger picture of your life is also not in harmony. Remember to attend to your own particular context—you don't have to achieve gigantic goals in order to move forward on your path. If there have been big changes in your life—such as entering a new school, having a child, or starting a new job—that have shifted your focus heavily into one domain, you'll naturally need to focus more effort there. But you can still stay on your path in the other domains; you just might need to reevaluate how you prioritize your goals and activities. If this resonates with you, then contemplate the ways you could travel on your path in more of the domains of your life, perhaps just moving a bit more slowly and simply focusing on being more present in the here and now when you have time to spend there.

You may also need to reorient yourself and make some changes in other ways if you're feeling like your life is not in harmony. Is your pull toward one domain of life actually a subtle avoidance of other domains? For example, Cal justified focusing on gourmet food for their children as a parenting value, but it actually functioned to keep them from addressing real and meaningful challenges in their valued career domain. There may also be problematic factors keeping you focused on one part of your life to the detriment of others. A workplace culture of long hours and weekend work will limit your time to do other activities, such as nurturing an intimate, burgeoning relationship with a significant other. The question isn't just whether you should or shouldn't work overtime or spend time with your new partner, but also whether it's helping you to be where you want to be in the big picture of your life. Only you can answer that question, and it's one worth sincere reflection. Spending a lot of time in only one domain should ideally be a conscious choice, not just something you do because of societal expectations.

We have also alluded to more serious issues, such as toxic relationships or work environments leading to burnout and psychological distress, and clinically relevant behavioral health concerns. The MAP can *help* support you in taking action with these issues, but it's not designed to be used on its own in such cases. We hope, if you're facing one of these issues, that you're already seeking assistance from a professional who is providing you with a reliable and impactful intervention approach. The MAP can guide you by providing support for committing to this intervention. If the reflections in this book have led to serious concerns, and you do not yet have professional support, we urge you to prioritize self-care on your to-do list, in service of all the values you have identified as bringing your life meaning and purpose.

Whatever your current context, you now have effective tools for leading a value-directed life, thriving rather than just surviving, and appreciating the landscape around you as you move forward on your path. We wish you well on your journey.

References

Association for Contextual Behavior Science (ACBS). n.d. "About ACBS." Accessed May 7, 2022. https://contextualscience.org/acbs.

A-Tjak, J. G. L., M. L. Davis, N. Morina, M. B. Powers, J. A. J. Smits, and P. M. Emmelkamp. 2015. "A Meta-Analysis of the Efficacy of Acceptance and Commitment Therapy for Clinically Relevant Mental and Physical Health Problems." *Psychotherapy and Psychosomatics* 84, no. 30: 30–36.

Amini Naghani S., S. Najarpourian, and S. A. Samavi. 2020. "Comparing the Effectiveness of the Triple P-Positive Parenting Program and Parenting Program of Acceptance and Commitment Therapy on Parent-Child Relationship and Self-Efficacy of Mothers with Oppositional Defiant Disorder Children." *Journal of Research and Health* 10, no. 2: 111–22.

Azimifar, S., M. Fatehizadeh, F. Bahrami, A. Ahmadi, and A. Abedi. 2016. "Comparing the Effects of Cognitive-Behavioral Couple Therapy & ACT on Marital Happiness of Dissatisfied Couples." *The Shenakht Journal of Psychology and Psychiatry* 3, no. 2: 56–81.

Bricker, J. B., B. M. Sullivan, K. E. Mull, A. J. Torres, and K. M. Carpenter. 2022. "Full-Scale Randomized Trial Comparing Acceptance and Commitment Therapy (ACT) Telephone-Delivered Coaching with Standard Telephone-Delivered Coaching Among Medicare/ Uninsured Quitline Callers." *Nicotine & Tobacco Research.* https://doi.org/10.1093/ntr/ntac052.

Bu, D., P. Chung, C. Zhang, and J. Liu. 2020. "The Effect of Mindfulness Training on Mental Health in Chinese Elite Badminton Players: A Randomized Controlled Trial. *Chinese Journal of Sports Medicine* 39, no. 12: 944–52.

Cho, H. A. 2013. "The Effect of Acceptance and Commitment Therapy (ACT) on Interpersonal Relationship Stress of Low-Income Children. *Korean Journal of Counseling* 14, no. 6: 3811–28.

Ciarrochi, J., L. Bilich, and C. Godsell. 2010. "Psychological Flexibility as a Mechanism of Change in Acceptance and Commitment Therapy." In *Assessing Mindfulness and Acceptance Processes in*

Clients: Illuminating the Theory and Practice of Change, ed. R. A. Baer, 51–75. Oakland, CA: Context Press/New Harbinger Publications.

Dindo, L., J. G. Fiedorowicz, D. M. Boykin, N. Wooldridge, J. Myers, T. Ajibewa, A. Stroud, D. Kuwaye, Z. Liu, and G. L. Pierce. 2021. "A Randomized Controlled Trial for Symptoms of Anxiety and Depression: Effects of a 1-Day Acceptance and Commitment Training Workshop. *Annals of Clinical Psychiatry,* 33, no. 4: 258–69.

Endsley, M. R., S. J. Selcon, T. D. Hardiman, and D. G. Croft. 1998. "A Comparative Analysis of SAGAT and SART for Evaluations of Situation Awareness." In *Proceedings of the Human Factors and Ergonomics Society 42nd Annual Meeting* 42, no. 1: 82–86. Santa Monica, CA: The Human Factors and Ergonomics Society.

Faryabi, M., A. Rafieipour, K. H. Alizadeh, and S. Khodavardian. 2021. "Comparison of the Effectiveness of Cognitive-Behavioral Therapy and Acceptance and Commitment Therapy on Anxiety, Perceived Stress, and Pain Coping Strategies in Patients with Cancer." *International Journal of Body, Mind and Culture* 8, no. 1: 61–71.

Flaxman, P. E., F. W. Bond, and F. Livheim. 2013. *The Mindful and Effective Employee: An Acceptance and Commitment Therapy Training Manual for Improving Well-Being and Performance.* Oakland, CA: New Harbinger Publications.

Gawande, A. 2009. *The Checklist Manifesto: How to Get Things Right.* New York: Henry Holt and Company.

Hayes, S. C., K. D. Strosahl, and K. G. Wilson. 2012. *Acceptance and Commitment Therapy: The Process and Practice of Mindful Change.* 2nd ed. New York: Guilford Press.

Hayes, S. C., R. D. Zettle, and I. Rosenfarb. 1989. "Rule-Following." In *Rule-Governed Behavior: Cognition, Contingencies, and Instructional Control,* ed. S. C. Hayes, 191–220. New York: Plenum Press.

Ii, T., H. Sato, N. Watanabe, M. Kondo, A. Masuda, S. C. Hayes, and T. Akechi. 2019. "Psychological Flexibility-Based Interventions Versus First-Line Psychosocial Interventions for Substance Use Disorders: Systematic Review and Meta-analyses of Randomized Controlled Trials. *Journal of Contextual Behavioral Sciences* 13: 109–20.

Ivanova, E., N. Yaakoba-Zohar, D. Jensen, J. Cassoff, and B. Knauper. 2016. "Acceptance and Commitment Therapy and Implementation Intentions Increase Exercise Enjoyment and Long-Term Exercise Behavior Among Low-Active Women. *Current Psychology* 35: 108–14.

Kangasniemi, A. M., R. Lappalainen, A. Kankaanpää, A. Tolvanen, and T. Tammelin. 2015. "Towards a Physically More Active Lifestyle Based on One's Own Values: The Results of a Randomized Controlled Trial Among Physically Inactive Adults." *BMC Public Health* 15: 260.

Kelson, J., A. Rollin, B. Ridout, and A. Campbell. 2019. "Internet-Delivered Acceptance and Commitment Therapy for Anxiety Treatment: Systematic Review. *Journal of Medical Internet Research* 21, no. 1: e12530.

Killingsworth, M. A., and D. T. Gilbert. 2010. "A Wandering Mind Is an Unhappy Mind. *Science* 303: 931–32.

Lillis, J., S. Dunsiger, J. G. Thomas, K. M. Ross, and R. R. Wing. 2021. "Novel Behavioral Interventions to Improve Long-Term Weight Loss: A Randomized Trial of Acceptance and Commitment Therapy or Self-Regulation for Weight Loss Maintenance." *Journal of Behavioral Medicine* 44, no. 4: 527–40.

Lundgren, T., G. Reinebo, M. J. Fröjmark, E. Jäder, M. Näslund, P. Svartvadet, U. Samuelsson, and T. Parling. 2021. "Acceptance and Commitment Training for Ice Hockey Players: A Randomized Controlled Trial. *Frontiers in Psychology* 12: 3097.

Ming, S., E. Gould, and J. Fiebig. 2023. *Understanding and Applying Relational Frame Theory: Complex Language as the Foundation of Our Work as Behavior Analysts.* Oakland, CA: New Harbinger Publications.

Moran, D. J. 2015. "Acceptance and Commitment Training in the Workplace. *Current Opinion in Psychology* 2: 26–31.

Paliliunas, D., J. Belisle, and M. R. Dixon. 2018. "A Randomized Control Trial to Evaluate the Use of Acceptance and Commitment Therapy (ACT) to Increase Academic Performance and Psychological Flexibility in Graduate Students. *Behavior Analysis in Practice* 11: 241–53.

Perkins, A., G. Bowers, J. Cassidy, R. Meiser-Stedman, and L. Pass. 2021. "An Enhanced Psychological Mindset Intervention to Promote Adolescent Wellbeing Within Educational Settings: A Feasibility Randomized Controlled Trial." *Journal of Clinical Psychology* 77: 946–67.

Piri, S., D. Hosseininasab, and S. Livarjani. 2020. "The Effectiveness of Acceptance and Commitment Therapy on Academic Procrastination, Resilience, and Depression in High School Male Students with Attention Deficit/Hyperactivity Disorder (ADHD). *Journal of Rehabilitation Medicine* 9, no. 4: 82–90.

Rosales-Villacrés, M. D. L., C. Oyanadel, D. Changotasig-Loja, and W. Peñate-Castro. 2021. "Effects of a Mindfulness and Acceptance-Based Program on Intimate Relationships in a Youth Sample: A Randomized Controlled Trial. *Behavioral Sciences* 11: 84.

Rose, M., C. D. Graham, N. O'Connell, C. Vari, V. Edwards, E. Taylor, L. M. McCracken, A. Radunovic, W. Rakowicz, S. Norton, and T. Chalder. 2022. "A Randomised Controlled Trial of Acceptance and Commitment Therapy for Improving Quality of Life in People with Muscle Diseases." *Psychological Medicine* 1–14. https://doi.org/10.1017/S0033291722000083.

Ruiz, F. J., and C. Luciano. 2012. "Improving International-Level Chess Players' Performance with an Acceptance-Based Protocol: Preliminary Findings. *The Psychological Record* 62: 447–62.

Saeidi, A., S. Jabalameli, Y. Gorji, and A. Ebrahimi. 2021. "Effect of Acceptance and Commitment Therapy on Self-Care and Psychological Capital of Patients with Diabetes. *Journal of Diabetes Nursing* 9, no. 3: 1633–47.

Shirazipour, M. M. 2022. "The Effectiveness of Treatment Based on Acceptance and Commitment to Reduce Rumination and Worry About Body Image of the Elderly with Depression." *Fundamentals of Mental Health* 24, no. 1: 21–28.

Swain, N., and S. Bodkin-Allen. 2017. "Developing Singing Confidence in Early Childhood Teachers Using Acceptance and Commitment Therapy and Group Singing: A Randomized Trial. *Research Studies in Music Education* 39: 109–20.

Yadavari, M., F. Naderi, and B. Makvandi. 2021. "The Effectiveness of Acceptance and Commitment Therapy on Depression, Anxiety, and Stress in Patients with Chronic Pain in Ahvaz." *International Journal of Health Studies* 7, no. 1: 28–32.

Yemm, G. 2013. *Financial Times Essential Guides—Leading Your Team: How to Set Goals, Measure Performance, and Reward Talent.* FT Publishing/Pearson. Kindle.

Daniel J. Moran, PhD, BCBA-D, is founder of Pickslyde Consulting, and associate professor at Touro University. His appearances on the Oprah Winfrey Network, The Learning Channel, and Discovery focused on discussing acceptance and commitment therapy (ACT) for people dealing with anxiety, depression, and substance-abuse concerns. In addition, he has successfully consulted with small start-up organizations and international Fortune 500 companies to ensure leaders and associates find their why and find their way.

Siri Ming, PhD, BCBA-D, is a scientist-practitioner with more than twenty-five years of experience in the field, and a commitment to the compassionate practice of behavior analysis to help people live meaningful, values-directed lives. Her research and clinical focus are on relational frame theory (RFT) and early language development, and she has authored numerous peer-reviewed research and theoretical articles, as well as a practical handbook on using RFT in early intervention programs for children with autism. She also provides support to clinicians and creatives to help them find and stay on their chosen path. Her work is grounded in the values of rigor, generosity, and kindness. Siri lives in Baltimore, MD.

MORE BOOKS from
NEW HARBINGER PUBLICATIONS

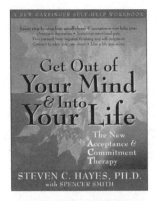
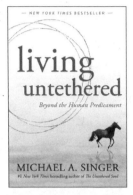
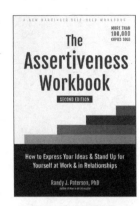

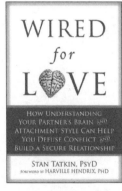

Real change *is* possible

For more than forty-five years, New Harbinger has published proven-effective self-help books and pioneering workbooks to help readers of all ages and backgrounds improve mental health and well-being, and achieve lasting personal growth. In addition, our spirituality books offer profound guidance for deepening awareness and cultivating healing, self-discovery, and fulfillment.

Founded by psychologist Matthew McKay and Patrick Fanning, New Harbinger is proud to be an independent, employee-owned company. Our books reflect our core values of integrity, innovation, commitment, sustainability, compassion, and trust. Written by leaders in the field and recommended by therapists worldwide, New Harbinger books are practical, accessible, and provide real tools for real change.

 newharbingerpublications

Did you know there are **free tools** you can download for this book?

Free tools are things like **worksheets**, **guided meditation exercises**, and **more** that will help you get the most out of your book.

You can download free tools for this book— whether you bought or borrowed it, in any format, from any source—from the New Harbinger website. All you need is a NewHarbinger.com account. Just use the URL provided in this book to view the free tools that are available for it. Then, click on the "download" button for the free tool you want, and follow the prompts that appear to log in to your NewHarbinger.com account and download the material.

You can also save the free tools for this book to your **Free Tools Library** so you can access them again anytime, just by logging in to your account!

Just look for this button on the book's free tools page. ➤

> **+ Save this to my free tools library**

If you need help accessing or downloading free tools, visit **newharbinger.com/faq** or contact us at **customerservice@newharbinger.com**.